295

ASIA'S
New Industrial World

ASIA'S New Industrial World

MICHAEL SMITH
JANE McLOUGHLIN
PETER LARGE
ROD CHAPMAN

METHUEN

LONDON AND NEW YORK

First published in 1985 by
Methuen & Co. Ltd
11 New Fetter Lane
London EC4P 4EE

Published in the USA by
Methuen & Co.
in association with Methuen, Inc.
733 Third Avenue
New York, NY 10017

Typeset by
Scarborough Typesetting Services
and printed in Great Britain by
Richard Clay (The Chaucer Press) Ltd,
Bungay, Suffolk

British Library Cataloguing in
Publication Data

Asia's new industrial world.
1. Asia – Industries
I. Smith, Michael, 1947 Apr. 10–
338.095   HC412

ISBN 0–416–38920–1

Library of Congress Cataloging in
Publication Data

Main entry under title:

Asia's new industrial world.
1. Japan – Industries – Addresses,
essays, lectures.
2. Korea (South) – Industries –
Addresses, essays, lectures.
3. Singapore – Industries –
Addresses, essays, lectures.
I. Smith, Michael, 1946–
HC462.9.A843   1985   338.095
84–27273

ISBN 0–416–38920–1

CONTENTS

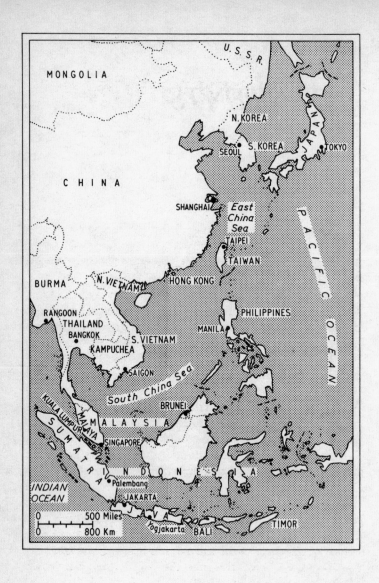

INTRODUCTION

Perhaps we should blame Alexander the Great or Marco Polo. It was these remarkable men, after all, who first brought the mysterious Orient to the attention of the West and we have been captivated since. Alexander it was who broke free from the Mediterranean world, striking east into Asia more than 2000 years ago. By the thirteenth century, the Polo family of explorers, notably Marco Polo, had plunged more deeply into the vast Asian continent and brought back wondrous tales of the East. There followed more exploration and, inevitably, exploitation as Western nations like Britain, Portugal, Holland and America colonized large tracts of the continent.

Today the West's fascination with the East is no longer restricted to its strange customs or different culture. Today the West is learning how to exist and compete with an area of the world which economically and industrially is gearing up to dominate the planet in the twenty-first century.

If the nineteenth century was Europe's and the twentieth century America's, will the twenty-first become the Far East's century? It was this most difficult of questions which set us four off on our 60,000 mile search for first-hand clues. What we came back with was a story – perhaps in ways as fascinating as some Marco Polo brought back to the

West all those centuries ago – of a continent which has played an increasingly significant part in reshaping the world's industrial map in recent decades and now stands poised for further major growth and development. It is a story which the West should not ignore.

Our mission took us to four key centres of Asia:

1   Japan, a fiercely proud country that has rebuilt itself since the war and is now second only to the mighty United States in economic power. Japan's ambition, though, is to become No. 1 and a huge national effort of resources and people is being mobilized to achieve that goal.
2   Korea, a divided nation that placed its faith in post-war recovery firmly into the smokestack heavy industries of steel, motor cars and shipbuilding. But South Korea is now deep in transition, searching for new technologies and a new role.
3   Singapore, once a colonial outpost and now in potentially formidable mid-development of 'brain' industries. Singapore holds the richest of all assets for success in the coming, de-industrialized world: the asset of having nothing – no long-standing heavy industry to restrain its growth and no natural resources like oil to provide a cushion. Instead, Singapore is investing in its people.
4   Indonesia is a rarity in the Far East, being a nation which can boast its own natural resources – the black gold of oil. Indonesia, a member of the Organization of Petroleum Exporting Countries cartel, OPEC, is probably the least developed of our chosen four and the one which most obviously stands at the crossroads of its development.

Although strikingly disparate in many respects, the four nations share many things in common. Some, like Japan and South Korea, emerged from the ashes of war to rebuild their shattered countries on heavy, mass production industries, starting in the shipyards and steel works and moving into sweat shop electronics. Today, though, all four share the common thirst for knowledge – particularly the knowledge of the new technologies like electronics and bio-technology. Brain is fast replacing brawn.

This thirst for knowledge and understanding has prompted a joint recognition by all four countries of the need for a vast investment in education, particularly higher education, and research and development. Singapore, for example, is now producing more computer science and electronics graduates, *pro rata*, than Britain, and one research and development worker in every eight throughout the world is Japanese.

Significantly, the three most advanced of the quartet countries – Japan, South Korea and Singapore – have all developed and grown with the aid of an unusual economic climate. Each of their economies is founded solidly on the basis of rampant free market competition, where only the fittest survive. But sitting astride this intensely competitive arena, all three have developed a rare degree of central economic planning between government and industry that smacks of a corporate state. It is an odd cocktail, mixing free market competition with corporate state consensus planning – but in the Far East it works.

It works because, generally speaking, the people in the Far East embrace consensus and compromise as a natural way of life and an acceptable means of making progress for the benefit of all. It is often a case of consensus rather than confrontation, backed up by the traditional Asian values of hard work and frugality. So far this overall mixture has proved to be a formidable combination and one which has laid the foundations for the future development of the region.

The four countries have, to a very large extent, an in-built resilience and a driving passion to succeed. They can support their mission by summoning up the huge resources from post-war economic growth and development and, their ultimate weapon, the awesome national consensus among their people.

The twenty-first century is not very far away.

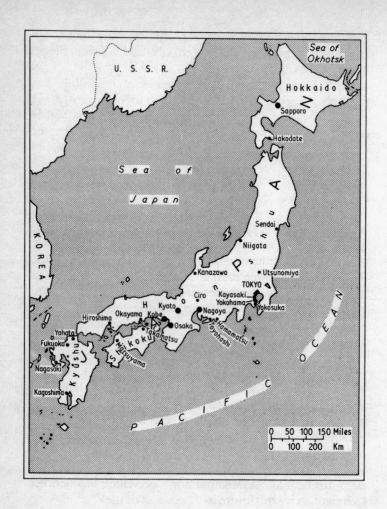

1 *JAPAN*

MICHAEL SMITH

Japan is unquestionably the most potent force in the Asian world. But this country, which has risen from the ashes of two atomic bombs and utter devastation in World War II, now nurses two ambitions – to be *ichi ban* (number one) and to be loved and respected. It is a formidable combination of objectives which perhaps only a truly formidable nation like Japan could ever possibly hope to achieve.

From the Japanese standpoint, the drive to become the world's foremost industrial nation is seen as a way of achieving the goal of global respect for which the Japanese population itself so obviously craves. But the more cynical West responds by saying that one does not necessarily produce the other. Undeterred, Japan is setting about the task of becoming number one with a degree of collective commitment and forward planning which leaves the West looking distinctly pedestrian.

In their bid to succeed the Japanese can call on one price-less asset not available to most other countries – a chilling degree of national consensus. Their sense of collective will and commitment is easily aroused and directed, yet it cannot appear in economic equations and forecasts. Indeed, the national consensus in Japan can make much of the economic soothsaying totally redundant.

The Japanese worker and the work culture of Japan provide the country with a head start in the race for supremacy. The Japanese worker is undoubtedly more committed than his or her counterpart in Britain, America or even West Germany. The work ethic remains a powerful influence in Japan. The result is that the work ethic combines potently with the easily aroused national consensus to produce a work culture where everyone in a company, from the top to the bottom, knows his or her correct place and, perhaps most important of all, they can all pull more smoothly in the same direction.

The Japanese undoubtedly feel most comfortable when they conform with each other. This, like so much of Japanese life, is contradictory, since the highly competitive style of educating, employing and trading, both domestically and internationally, makes Japanese society among the most aggressive in the world. Yet the Japanese people prefer to conform.

This consensus was perhaps most apparent immediately after the war as the Japanese began the enormous task of rebuilding their shattered country. Japan, more than any other nation, was able to mobilize its people to this essential task.

Initially, Japan rebuilt and expanded its industrial base, investing heavily in large, labour-intensive industries like steel-manufacturing and shipbuilding. It was the sense of collective purpose together with substantial investment which laid the foundations for what is now commonly known as the Japanese 'economic miracle'.

The need to export, to improve the nation's balance of payments, was a crucial feature of the early stages of Japan's development. So the government restricted the inflow of imported foreign goods and services like banking, made it more difficult for overseas companies to invest directly in Japan and energetically promoted Japanese export trade. Wedded to all these initiatives was the fact that the Japanese people are inveterate savers and the banks

Table 1.1 Japanese economic growth in the world economy: shares of GNP of major countries in the world

	1955 (%)	1960 (%)	1970 (%)	1978 (%)	1980 (%)
Japan	2.2	2.9	6.0	10.0	9.0
USA	36.3	33.7	30.2	21.8	21.5
EEC	17.5	17.5	19.3	20.2	22.4
USSR	13.9	15.2	15.9	13.0	11.6
China	4.4	4.7	4.9	4.6	4.7
Others	25.7	26.0	23.7	30.4	30.8
World's total	100.0	100.0	100.0	100.0	100.0
($ billion)	(1,100)	(1,500)	(3,250)	(9,660)	(12,215)

Source: Economic Planning Agency.

provided ordinary people with one of the few places in which to deposit their savings. As the economy grew, Japanese workers became more prosperous and channelled their money into the banks, and the banks readily lent their expanding resources to an expanding industrial machine. It was simple, but effective.

Japan's gross domestic product (GDP) grew at an average of 10.5 per cent between 1950 and 1973, compared with a worldwide growth rate of 4.7 per cent over the same period. Even after the 1973 oil shock, which had a dire effect on the economy because the country imports all its oil requirements, Japan fared much better than most others in the world. Japan's GDP advanced by an average of 4.7 per cent in the following years while its trading rivals were growing at half the rate.

But Japan later became a victim of its own miracle. Europe and America reacted badly to Japan's increasing dominance of world markets in key areas like motor vehicles, computers and steel, and protectionist trade barriers were erected. The West was particularly concerned that Japan concentrated its attack on a limited number of export markets, such as cars and steel, while Western

Table 1.2 GNP and GNP per capita (1980) and growth rate of GNP (1971–80)

	GNP (nominal)[a]		Annual growth rate (real)	
	(US$ billion)	Per capita (US$)	1971–5 (%)	1976–80 (%)
USA	2,626.1	11,535	2.6	3.7
Japan	1,035.8	8,870	4.7	5.0
Germany, FR	820.8	13,333	2.1	3.6
France	656.0	12,214	4.0	3.3
UK	523.6	9,359	2.0	1.4
Italy	396.5	6,951	4.1	3.8
Canada	253.3	10,582	5.0	3.0
Brazil	237.4	1,929	10.8	6.5[c]
Netherlands	167.6	11,855	3.2	2.5
Australia	148.2	10,135	3.4	2.5
India	133.6[b]	205[b]	2.9	2.9
Sweden	122.6	14,771	2.7	1.2

Source: Bank of Japan, *Comparative International Statistics*, 1982.

Notes: (a) US dollar figures are calculated according to the annual exchange rates of the IMF, *International Financial Statistics*. (b) 1979. (c) 1976–9.

exporters were more catholic in the goods they sold abroad. In addition, the West has argued with some effect that their companies are not able to sell goods into Japan as easily as Japanese exporters are able to manufacture for the West.

The protectionist tendencies of the West have combined with a slowdown in what was previously regarded as Japan's insatiable appetite for consumer goods to produce more modest economic growth. Today Japan is expanding at a rate nearer to 2.5–3 per cent compared with over 10 per cent during the miracle years.

Cautious Japanese economists now regard the country's economy as close to maturity, which means that while heavy industries like steel and motor manufacturing will remain the bedrock, Japan must now seek to conquer entirely new areas of technological development. The West will be hoping that the demand for technology will increase Japan's appetite for Western goods and skills.

As long ago as the 1960s and early 1970s, however, the Japanese authorities were beginning to realize the need to diversify the industrial base and in particular the long-term potential of the new, or brain-intensive, industries such as electronics. Japan immediately began to lift the controls on certain imports and to attract new – and mostly other countries' – technology and know-how. It was then that Japan gained its reputation as a country which took other people's technology and put it to better use than the inventors.

The slow process of change was overtaken by the 1973 oil shock which forced Japan, a huge importer of oil, to speed up its industrial revolution. The massive rise in world oil prices drove up the costs of Japan's 'old' industries like steel, shipbuilding and textiles and whittled away the advantage of cheap labour costs.

It was crucial that the Japanese began to promote industrial change, rather than simply to protect struggling industries as so many countries in the West, including Britain, chose to do. Steps were taken to conserve energy and promote an orderly reduction in production capacity in certain industries like steel, and incentives were devised to encourage the growth and development of the new industries like electronics.

This process of structural change gathered pace as Japan stepped up its capital expenditure by huge sums during the 1970s. As a result, Japanese industrial output soared by 50 per cent between 1975 and 1982, well above the average growth seen elsewhere in the advanced industrialized world. During this period production by traditional and often heavy energy-using industries like steel and petrochemicals failed to grow while the new areas like electronics, assembling and processing industries began to expand fast.

It was then that the West first began to appreciate the implications of the structural change taking place in Japan's industrial base – from smokestack industries to shirt-sleeved brain industries.

*

Kazihiro Fuchi is a typical Japanese. He is small, be-spectacled and energetic. He is also a towering symbol of the new Japan, a new industrial nation where brain is replacing brawn.

Fuchi, now in his late 40s, works in a busy office, high up in a Tokyo skyscraper, leading a small, select team of scientists and electronics engineers trying to build a super-computer. The project, the most technologically advanced computer development ever, is known as the Fifth Generation computer.

Fuchi and his earnest-looking colleagues, who sit hunched over desks and terminals in the Tokyo tower block, are aiming to build computers that can do things they were previously thought incapable of doing. The Fifth Generation project aims to break new ground in the delicate field of artificial intelligence, which essentially means creating a computer that can think for itself. Spin-offs include a typewriter mechanism that can react to human speech and an automatic translating machine.

To Japan, however, the Fifth Generation is a great deal more than another piece of 'gee-whiz' technological development. The project has virtually become a virility symbol for a nation which is desperate to prove itself to a sceptical world. Japan has set itself the national goal of building a Fifth Generation computer by 1993, and if Fuchi and his small team succeed in beating the Americans and the Europeans, they will have given Japan an enormous 'coming of age' present.

Traditionally, the pioneering work in computers has been done by American or European scientists and engineers. Perhaps it is a sense of pique that prompts some in the West to talk of the Japanese Fifth Generation project as an 'electronic Pearl Harbor'.

However, the Japanese firmly believe that the successful development of the Fifth Generation will demonstrate to the world once and for all that Japan is perfectly capable of developing its own technology. Few things upset people like Kazihiro Fuchi more than the customary Western jibe that Japan has succeeded only by acquiring other people's technology. The Fifth Generation project will demonstrate that Japan, too, can innovate in a big way.

The drive for computer superiority is also a classic case study of how the Japanese are fast diverting their economic base away from traditional heavy industry into newer and brain technologies, where knowledge is a more potent tool than being able to build ships more cheaply than international competitors.

It is an equally classic case study of how the consensus between business and government works in Japan, even though the national economy is a monetarist's dream of rampant free markets and modest government interference. Private industry and commerce dictate industrial policy, though in practice the government and its agencies, such as the powerful Ministry for International Trade and Industry (MITI), take a major part in shaping long-term planning. It is a curious marriage of unbridled free competition and a centrally planned corporate state. Most countries make do with one or the other, or at least a predominance of one.

Yet in Japan the marriage clearly works, mainly because the people are devoted to the principle of consensus. To outsiders, the easily aroused and potentially easily manipulated sense of collective will is both awesome in its power and chilling if directed by the wrong hands. In either form it comes naturally to the ordinary Japanese.

The consensus between politics and business is perfectly illustrated by the Fifth Generation project. In the early 1980s Japanese computer firms and computer scientists approached the government with a plea for assistance to develop the Fifth Generation project. Today, Fuchi and his scientists and engineers are backed by £300 million of government funds and have access to invaluable practical and technical assistance from the computer firms themselves.

The computer industry provides the brains and facilities and the government provides the cash. At the end of the day, the results of Fuchi's work will be passed back to the firms. By the early 1990s the many scientists who were seconded to work on the Fifth Generation project during the 1980s will be putting their work to practical effect in their own companies like Toshiba, Hitachi and Fujitsu.

In the case of the Fifth Generation computer project, the link between the corporate state as represented by MITI and the free market forces of the giant computer-manufacturing companies is a marriage of convenience. Individual firms could not afford the £300 million development costs, nor would they wish to commit themselves to a 10–15-year research programme, which might divert resources and people away from the short-term considerations of the market place. Equally, a government department like MITI could not consider undertaking a massive research project without establishing its own facilities and personnel, especially as private industry in Japan pays a great deal more in wages than government agencies.

So the government provides the money and the platform, industry comes up with the researchers from all the private companies, and Japan Inc. will eventually reap the benefits.

The Fifth Generation development model is being used in other areas where Japan is trying to shift from mass-production industries to brain-intensive fields. While private industry will finance the lion's share of the country's prodigious expenditure on research and development (R & D), the government is happy to pay for specialist projects, like the Fifth Generation computer development. But the government also ensures that key industrialists, financiers, academics and politicians are all involved in the planning process.

Not surprisingly, Japan's overall expenditure on R & D is now among the largest in the world and is growing fast. By 1981 Japan was spending £17 billion a year on R & D, equal to 2.4 per cent of the gross national product (GNP). This was only 0.1 per cent less than America, and Japan is scheduled to raise its share of R & D spending to 3 per cent of GNP by the middle of the 1980s, potentially making Japan the second largest R & D investor in the world.

Japanese R & D spending is different in two crucial aspects to that of most other advanced countries. First, the Japanese spend less than 1 per cent of their R & D budget on defence, and second, contrary to widespread belief, the government itself spends less on R & D than most Western nations. By the early 1980s, over 60 per cent of national R & D expenditure was being undertaken by industry, and the proportion is growing each year. Japan can now muster an army of almost 700,000 full-time research workers, equal to 1 for every 8 researchers throughout the world and more than all those employed in Britain, West Germany and France put together.

The Japanese government's funding of the R & D effort is now running at 25 per cent of the total expenditure, but this proportion is declining almost every year as private industry ploughs increasingly large sums into R & D. More than one-third of American R & D is financed by the government and the proportion in Britain, 32 per cent, is only slightly smaller.

Industry has consistently raised its share of the R & D outlay over the past decade, partly because of government tax incentives and partly because Japanese public companies tend to pay smaller dividends to shareholders and therefore companies have larger retained profits to re-invest in the business. It can safely be assumed that the Japanese government's proportion of the R & D budget will continue to decline in the coming years as private industry, driven by fierce internal and international competition, increases its expenditure on new technologies.

*

The essential fuel for the engine room of Japanese innovation is the country's education system which, quite simply, produces children with the highest Intelligence Quotient (IQ) in the world today. More important from the Japanese point of view, though, is the fact that the education system is widely regarded as being one of the key ingredients of the country's postwar industrial resurgence and one of the basic reasons why Japan is confidently expected to maintain its growth and development into new fields during the coming decades.

Japanese education inevitably reflects the country and people. The Japanese are by nature hungry for education, and the education system, like most things in the Japanese lifestyle, is basically aggressive. Even entrance to kindergarten is described as 'competitive'.

Japanese education underwent a substantial change in the 1960s as the authorities sought to devise a system which, for the long term, would 'meet the future progress of our country and society'. And as one observer from Britain has noted, the real culture shock of the Japanese education system in relation to our own is that the Japanese actually practise what they preach.

The Japanese, it must be said, have a near obsession with education, largely because the recruitment process of commerce and industry is geared very positively towards those leaving the higher education system. Employers have a strong influence on the education system and their main objective is that the schools turn out intelligent, not necessarily highly specialized, young people. There is, for example, no real tradition of careers teaching in schools.

Instead, Japanese schools focus their main attention on the fundamentals of education, notably the English equivalent of the three Rs. The aim, said one expert, is to mix academic and non-academic studies together and provide an education for the 'whole person'. Teachers, incidentally, are generally more respected as members of the community than in, say, Britain, and the Japanese national commitment to education is reflected in the fact that the government now sinks 10 per cent of the country's GNP into education.

The net result is that a massive 94 per cent of all children finish their compulsory education at 15 and move on to some other form of higher education or vocational training. Very few large employers would be prepared to recruit a 15-year-old straight from school. Britain, in contrast, is one of the few advanced industrialized nations where the vast majority of 16-year-old school-leavers are forced on to the labour market directly upon leaving school. In Japan, for example, the average age for starting work is 20.

Japan's emphasis on education and the advances being made are clearly illustrated by simple facts. In the early 1960s some 58 per cent of Japanese children moved on to higher education of some form after completing their formal education at 15 years of age. As we said above, the figure today is 94 per cent and only America can boast a higher turn-out. In the 1960s some 40 per cent of young Japanese went from school to work at the age of 15. Today, as we said, the figure is under 5 per cent.

In the 1960s around 8 per cent of school-leavers went on to university or the equivalent. In less than a generation the Japanese education system has pushed the percentage to 36 per cent and official estimates are that by the turn of the century it will have easily exceeded 40 per cent.

Because of the demands from industry, there is clearly a natural preference for the higher-education system to produce engineering and other specialist graduates. As recently as 1961 the Japanese were producing 20,000 engineering graduates. In 1984 the Japanese are turning out well over 70,000 engineering graduates a year and industry is understandably perfectly happy with the education system. In 1982, for example, the manufacturing industry in Japan recruited around 70,000 graduates and the construction industry picked up another 20,000.

As recently as 1968, 10 per cent of Japan's workforce had higher-education qualifications. A decade later the proportion had climbed to 15 per cent and by the turn of the century it is confidently expected that 25 per cent of all workers will have obtained some form of qualification from higher education.

Curiously, Japanese industry is not necessarily seeking young people highly skilled in one particular field. Employers, it seems, are less concerned about what their future employees know than how they are likely to learn and adapt to the demands of working life. Training is a regular feature of industrial life in Japan, even after qualification. Japanese industry is looking for young people who can think, learn and adapt, hence the concentration on producing a 'whole person'.

Japanese companies spend a great deal of time and money on training workers after they have joined the payroll. Precise figures are not available, but it is not unusual for a firm to invest 5 per cent of its annual sales turnover on training staff. This relatively high level of commitment to staff training partly reflects the Japanese companies' pledge to provide lifelong employment but it also reflects the national hunger for knowledge. So also does the fact that education and training in industry do not necessarily come to an end once a person has achieved one type of skill or expertise. Retraining and upgrading of skills are seen as no less an obligation than early initial training. Indeed, training in Japanese industry extends into other activities, such as the famous 'quality circles', where workers regularly participate in discussions to improve the design, manufacturing process and quality of a product. Although not strictly classified as training, the quality circles help build up the worker's skills and knowledge of his or her job.

The government's role in the education system should not be underestimated. Quite apart from providing huge sums of money for the system – 10 per cent of GNP – the government also creates an environment where education flourishes. Japan's Ministry of Labour plays a key role, regularly assessing the forthcoming trends in personnel supply and demand. By law the labour minister is required to draw up a five-year plan, known as the Vocational Training Plan, designed to assess workforce trends over the period, translate them into training requirements and promote measures to match the labour supply with industry's demands. The system is continuous and among other things has helped to anticipate critical gaps in Japan's labour market.

Significantly the Japanese have not allowed the impact of worldwide recession to divert the national education and industrial-training effort away from its goals. Education and training expenditure by the state has been maintained in the teeth of the recession and, as far as can be gauged, the outlay by private industry on training the labour force is actually on the increase.

Education, despite its massive contribution to past successes, still has its critics in Japan. There are those who say that students should specialize more and those who note that the Japanese system of technical colleges has not been a success from the employers' standpoint.

But whatever its disadvantages, there is no denying that the contribution it has made so far makes the Japanese education system one of the key factors in the country's economic resurgence. A bigger test will obviously come as Japan seeks to adapt to changed requirements and develop new skills and industry. But the pervading feeling in the country and the West is that Japan is now laying firm foundations to ensure that its past success can be largely repeated.

*

At the epicentre of this industrial and educational activity sits MITI, the Japanese government's powerful Ministry for

International Trade and Industry. MITI is probably the Japanese agency least understood yet most feared by those in the West. Surprisingly, MITI is a small organization, housed in humble surroundings and operating on a very modest annual budget of around £500 million, which is somewhat less than Britain spends annually on aid and assistance for the regions.

MITI's role is that of midwife and undertaker, nursing new industries and technological developments while at the same time co-ordinating the orderly run-down of ageing, decaying industries. MITI also provides the essential forum where government, industry, academics, financiers and trade unions can sit around the same table and shape the nation's industrial future. While MITI has not yet perfected the art of infallibility, the agency can claim to have had a profound influence in fashioning Japan's recent successful industrial developments and is now embarked on a new programme for the future.

The seemingly incompatible tasks of midwife and under-taker are performed through a series of 'talking shops' or councils, which promote informed debate on every imagin-able aspect of a particular industry, whether of its birth or its death. These councils call on key figures from the industry concerned, scientists and other academics, engin-eers, bankers and other financiers, and officials from differ-ent government ministries, including of course from MITI itself. MITI is consensus at work.

Another surprise about MITI, though, is that its influence today is perhaps not quite as strong as it was in the two decades immediately after the war. During that period of rebuilding, the Japanese depended heavily on their national sense of consensus and MITI was at the heart of the rebuild-ing programme.

However, MITI staged a comeback in the late 1970s when it became apparent that national consensus would be needed to steer the country into the 'brain industries' and to develop new technologies. MITI moved back into the spotlight, helping to complete the orderly run-down of some declining industries, but more particularly preparing the blueprint for the future.

A substantial part of MITI's work is still devoted to assisting the older, mainly energy-intensive industries like shipbuilding, man-made-fibre manufacturing and aluminium production. At the end of 1983, for example, MITI was caring for twenty-one separate industrial sectors, such as sugar refiners, fertilizer makers and petrochemical producers. Several more industries, including cement manufacture, are likely to join the MITI sick list during the rest of the decade. However, it is MITI's role in shaping new industrial patterns which represents the agency's most intriguing task.

MITI first became involved with the modern, futuristic industries back in 1957 when the agency helped to reorganize the country's computer manufacturers. By the 1970s MITI was again in full flight, helped by a new government directive that the country should embark on a rapid programme of development in the information- and machine-technology industries. MITI weighed in with some finance and a great deal of encouragement to those firms willing to explore the new territory.

Since then, there have been at least ten specific MITI projects related to the electronics industry alone, and MITI and related government agencies are engaged in a massive programme of promoting Japanese industry towards major developments in modern industries as far apart as nuclear fusion and biotechnology. In the key electronics industry, a notable MITI triumph was to help firms to develop the big new microchips for the new range of modern computers and Japan today sells over 70 per cent of these 64K random access memory chips.

By 1981 MITI had drawn up a new and still more impressive set of targets, known officially as the project for the development of fundamental technologies for the 'next generation industries' – a phrase which sums up virtually all of Japan's present industrial policies. MITI explained: 'Its aim is to promote the development of the technologies now in their infancy to become effective industrial technologies and achieve their commercialization in ten years.' Together, the existing and new development projects being fostered by MITI represent a huge national effort to 'pick winners' for the future.

The thrust of the new developments will be found in Japan's search for high-technology supremacy – the development of microelectronics, new materials and biotechnology. According to Japanese estimates, the software users of the microelectronic products will become a £70 billion industry by the 1990s. The development of new materials, such as composites, which will start to replace heavier metals, will develop to a £30 billion industry by the year 2000, and biotechnology will be a £20 billion business by the turn of the century.

An essential part of current thinking is that Japan must develop its own technology, and stop relying on the West for knowledge. But there are serious doubts in MITI about whether the financial climate in Japan can possibly accommodate the scale of MITI's development plan for the late 1980s and beyond. Even MITI officials express these doubts, and successful completion of the programme will depend to a very large extent on the co-operation that MITI can win from the financial authorities and possibly from private-sector firms.

Japan appreciates the difficulty of the task and has already invited greater participation and co-operation from firms in the West. Increased co-operation provides the Japanese with greater access to advanced Western technology in several key areas, as well as overcoming the financial constraints on developing these resources single-handed. But such a policy has meant that some sections of Japanese society have had to stifle their strong nationalistic feelings and modify their view that Japan on its own can achieve anything it visualizes.

Some major steps have already been taken along the road to participation and co-operation. Following the economic summit meeting in Japan in 1983, the advanced industrialized nations drew up a 'hit list' of eighteen specific projects in which countries should participate to share in the development of new technologies. Japan, which was especially anxious to emphasize its ability to innovate, became the leader in 3 of the 18 projects and agreed to participate in a total of 13 developments.

The main thrust of the research projects, incidentally, had a distinctly Japanese flavour. One was to gain a greater insight into the practical use of solar power. If achieved, of course, development of a reliable, practical and economic source of solar-power generation would help ease Japan's heavy reliance on imported energy. Another very Japanese research project involved developing an advanced robot system, which would replace people in difficult or hostile work environments.

Japan has also been exerting its influence through official bodies like the International Energy Agency to generate greater urgency in the development of alternative sources of energy and improved conservation techniques. Both stem from the country's firm desire to solve its own domestic energy problems, but there is little doubt that the West too will benefit if the initiatives succeed.

More immediately, Japan has already begun to build up a substantial presence in key industries where previously it had limited knowledge and expertise. Obvious examples are aerospace and outer space.

Japanese aerospace companies have been anxious for some time to break into the big league of aircraft manufacturers and challenge the world supremacy of the American giants Boeing and McDonnell Douglas, and of Airbus Industrie, the four-nation European consortium. But virility symbols in the aerospace business come very expensive, and a cost of around £1 billion for the development of a new commercial passenger jet is too high – even for the ambitious Japanese.

One reason why the Japanese cannot find the resources to match those of the Americans or Europeans is that Japan is not permitted to export weapons of destruction, a stricture which obviously inhibits the growth of the country's aerospace industry on the scale seen in America or Europe. American aircraft-makers like Boeing and McDonnell Douglas supplement their commercial-jet building programmes with substantial orders and research contracts from the US Defence Ministry. Airbus receives massive financial support from the governments of Britain, France, West Germany and Spain to ensure that Europe has a viable aerospace industry to compete with the Americans.

Instead the Japanese have been concentrating on developing a series of work-sharing partnerships and technology exchanges with the acknowledged experts in America and Europe. And Japanese aerospace firms are eagerly searching for yet more tie-ups with the West to ensure that Japan has a substantial voice in the key aerospace industry in the 1990s and beyond. Japanese attention is focused mainly on America, partly because their unspoken ambition is eventually to compete on equal terms with Europe.

In true Japanese style the aerospace industry has embarked on the course of work-sharing partnerships and technology exchanges in a collective, orderly way. Monitored by the ever-watchful MITI, the emergence of Japan as a presence in the aerospace industry will be another triumph of consensus. Not surprisingly, the strategy is already working extremely well and Japan is moving from strength to strength.

The country's biggest collaborative venture is the participation in the V2500 aero-engine project, a five-nation programme aimed at producing the most technologically advanced aircraft engine ever at a cost of £1 billion. Japan's three main aero-engine firms – Ishikawajima-Harima Heavy Industries, Mitsubishi Heavy Industries and Kawasaki Heavy Industries – have formed a non-profit organization, the Japanese Aero Engines Corp., to handle the task. Japan has never before participated in such a commercial-aircraft engine project, and if successfully developed, it will give the country's aerospace firms a stake in a product likely to sell for at least two decades.

Similarly, Fuji Heavy Industries, Kawasaki and Mitsubishi are currently combining to take a 15 per cent share in the building of Boeing's 767 passenger jet. Japan's first-ever stake in the building of a commercial aircraft on this scale has been so successful that the firms have been able to repay MITI a large slice of the development costs, and the companies are now anxious to raise their shareholding in the project to a more substantial 25 per cent.

There are several other aerospace participation deals already in operation and many more under active negotiation. But the aerospace industry at present remains firmly wedded to the domestic defence industry, which still provides around three-quarters of its work. However, the obvious success of the Japanese in participating with the industry's giants will, it is hoped, unlock the door to large-scale expansion into international defence manufacturing. It is a prospect fraught with obvious worries. The stark memory of Japan's aggressive expansionism in the 1930s and 1940s, culminating in the Pacific War, will take a very long time to erase. It is this, perhaps more than anything else, which has led to the West's lingering distrust of the Japanese, even in peacetime.

But Japanese aerospace executives are quietly confident that the industry is going to expand in a big way. There is a firm belief that the development of commercial aircraft, defence manufacture and more recently space technology will propel the Japanese aerospace industry into very serious competition with Europe by the turn of the century.

All the groundwork is now being laid and this huge development, if it comes off, will have been achieved almost entirely through joint ventures, work-sharing agreements and technology exchanges – all under the watchful eye of MITI and the national consensus.

*

Japan's industrial resurgence since the end of World War II has passed through two distinct phases and is now in the middle of a third. In the late 1950s and the 1960s Japan rebuilt its economy with smokestack, mass-production industries like steel, motor cars and shipbuilding. By the 1970s the emphasis had switched to the more intricate manufacture of consumer goods like pocket calculators, colour televisions and hi-fi equipment. Today Japan is passing through a crucial phase of establishing its credentials in the age of new technologies, like microchips, computers and robots, and more important, laying the foundations for the fourth stage of its development.

There is little doubt – either inside Japan or in the West – that the burgeoning electronics industry will be the powerhouse for the country's continued growth and development in the coming decades. Japan's electronics industry is now roughly equal in size to its motor-manufacturing industry and all the forecasts point to continued substantial growth. But Japan is also seeking to establish significant manufacturing facilities in areas like computers, biotechnology, aerospace, pharmaceuticals, new raw materials to replace metals, nuclear power and lasers.

Japan is in a powerful position to exploit the opportunities for growth in the electronics industry because the postwar boom in calculators, televisions and more recently video recorders provided the domestic industry with enormous wealth and strength. The electronics industry in Japan is concentrated in a relatively small number of hands, but those hands have become powerful enough to finance the massive expansion that has made the industry the size it is today.

Looking ahead, however, experts in Japan believe that there will be a slight drift away from the electronics industry's strong consumer base. Instead, it is widely expected that future growth will come in the shape of growing industrial markets, like office automation, computers and computer equipment, and telecommunications. The consumer will continue to be a major, if slightly less important, customer in the future.

Industry estimates are that the value of electronics industry equipment will more than double from 1981 to well over £7.5 billion a year by 1990. If achieved, this will represent a remarkable average annual growth rate of 9.9 per cent. Significantly, the value of equipment for use in manufacturing is expected to grow at an annual average of more than 13 per cent compared with a very modest 3.1 per cent for consumer goods. This forecast reinforces the belief that industry is fast catching up the consumer as the largest customer of the electronics industry.

Not surprisingly, the fastest growth in the remaining years of the 1980s is anticipated by computer manufacturers, who expect an average annual growth of more than 17 per cent by the 1990s. Demand for office equipment and electronic parts, such as capacitors and magnetic tapes, is also expected to rocket in the next few years.

The rapidly expanding electronics industry will provide Japan with the scope to maintain a huge domestic industry while continuing to exploit export opportunities. This strategy has formed the basis of much of Japan's past economic expansion and is nowhere better illustrated than by the country's development of the special 64K microchip – so called because it stores 64,000 bits of information.

In the late 1970s the electronics firms centralized their research under the wing of government agencies to develop a new and technologically superior microchip for use in the larger computers then built. Western microchip firms were astonished when Japanese combines like the Nippon Electric Corporation plunged into mass production of the chips well ahead of rivals in America. Their boldness paid off and by the early 1980s the Japanese commanded a 70 per cent stake of the world market in 64K chips, worth a cool £650 million a year – and growing.

Today the same firms are seeking to repeat their coup by developing an even larger chip, the 256K, which can store 256,000 items of information and will be heavily in demand in the late 1980s. But will Western manufacturers, beaten to the punch so recently, lose out again? Time will tell.

Western firms can attempt to compete in the field of microchips because of the international nature of the product. But there will be little that they can do to counteract another Japanese innovation that threatens to further undermine Western industrial strength in another important field – information technology.

The thrust of Japan's new drive into the area of information technology is in the application in people's homes of systems like cable networks, direct broadcasting satellites, telecommunications and videotex. If adopted, a central, home-based computer will offer services like home shopping as well as being able to warn of disasters like fires, or simply adjust room temperatures and lighting to suit particular needs. The West has labelled the operation 'interactive home systems', and if widely practised it will lift new technology out of the textbooks and into millions of Japanese homes.

The rapid expansion of the information technology industry has other repercussions. For example, the main electronics companies in Japan have agreed to use a common standard home computer in interactive home systems. Overnight this will create a substantial new market for small home computers and the vast amount of software they will generate.

Equally there will be a dramatic expansion in the demand for cable systems, satellite hardware and software and videotex equipment to support interactive home systems.

More immediately, the state-owned Nippon Telegraph and Telephone Corporation is planning a new information network system (INS) to replace the existing telephone network. INS can provide the comprehensive communication of voices, information and even pictures.

The expected huge expansion in the domestic information technology industry will place Japanese electronics firms in an even more powerful position to compete with Western firms in world markets in the coming decades while also, of course, providing Japanese undertakings with increased wealth to research and develop new ideas.

Development on this scale will undoubtedly have side-effects. A report by MITI has estimated that development of the micro-electronics industry will cut the number of jobs in the machinery industry by up to 480,000 people, while those in department stores will be reduced by as many as 40,000. On the other hand, MITI estimates that the micro-electronics industry will generate between 200,000 and 720,000 new jobs.

Outside advancements in the electronics industry, the main areas of development in Japanese industry in the coming years will hardly be visible to the ordinary citizen. But Japan's long-term planners are setting great store by proposed developments in nuclear power, the creation of new raw materials, biotechnology and drug manufacture. While it is obviously difficult to generalize about a diverse range of products and applications, the one point which all these have in common is the relatively small scale of operations at present. Japan has none the less set high targets.

In 1981, for example, as we said, MITI drew up a new set of development targets for several important new fields of endeavour, a ten-year programme known as the project for the development of fundamental technologies for the next generation industries. The programme, backed by a nearly £300 million research budget, aims to commercialize the manufacture of tougher fine ceramics and polymers capable of substituting for aluminium, copper and other metals. Composite materials which are lighter and stronger than metals like aluminium are also being developed, and there are several projects to learn more about the commercial application of advances in biotechnology.

The search for alternative materials to a variety of metals is clearly one area where the Japanese are hoping to gain some competitive advantage over the West. Composites, for example, offer exciting opportunities for aircraft and space-systems manufacturers. Composite materials, which are made by combining a variety of materials like fibreglass, are much tougher and much lighter than conventional materials such as aluminium. The small scale of Japan's aerospace and space industries has stunted the growth of this new development. But composite-materials manufacturers have been gearing up for the future, and the suspicion is that Japan will play a large part in developing the industry as it expands beyond the more obvious areas like aircraft hulls, or even integrated circuits.

Biotechnology is another field where Japan is preparing for rapid expansion, though the commercialization of many developments may not take place until the 1990s. For the moment, there are strong hopes that 'biotech' advances will produce such breakthroughs as the anti-cancer drug or human growth hormones. By the 1990s Japan is hoping to have developed TPA – tissue plasminogen activator – which may remove a thrombosis. Potential worldwide sales from these applications will run into billions of pounds.

Looking a little further ahead, Japan is working on cell fusion and tissue culture advances in the hope of breeding new types of edible plants and replacing conventional plant breeding techniques.

Overall, the pattern has been established for this, the third, stage of Japan's industrial development – industry and government working closely together in projects as remote as the Fifth Generation Computer and anti-cancer applications from biotech breakthroughs. Industry will provide over three-quarters of the research expenditure while the government, through agencies like MITI, will selectively sprinkle the seed corn for tomorrow's industries.

The transition from the mass-produced, labour-intensive industries of the past is far from complete, and even when it is, there will still be a substantial role for 'old' industries like car manufacturing. But the change of emphasis, which began to take shape in the late 1970s and early 1980s, is now more pronounced than ever.

Today Japan's newer industries, like electronics and computers, biotechnology and aerospace, depend more on the skills and knowledge of the people involved in them. Industries of the future will demand more brain than brawn and Japan, with true precision, has laid the right foundations.

*

Long-term planning, allied to the national characteristic of consensus and a strong work ethic, has played a crucial role in determining Japan's economic success in the decades since the war. It may be, however, that the nation's undoubted ability to plan and prepare for change is the essential driving force behind the present pursuit of excellence and, most of all, the ambition to be *ichi ban* – number one.

For anyone with an ounce of understanding can see that, in spite of the postwar successes and the likely prizes which lie ahead in the future, Japan faces deep problems.

The most immediate problem is that the Japanese, like everyone else, are living in an era of slower economic growth. This slow-down has occurred at a time when Japan has become more reliant upon export trade to fuel its own economic growth, and the West – mainly through Europe and America – has been erecting protectionist barriers to shield its own declining industries. The West has a point. In 1981 the world trade in manufactured goods crawled ahead by only 2 per cent, but the volume of manufactured goods exported by Japan soared by 11 per cent. As a result, Japan has found markets in key export industries, like textiles, motor cars and certain consumer electronic goods such as video recorders, closed off or at best restricted.

Table 1.3 Japan's major trading partners (1981)*

(US$ million, except %)	Japan's exports to		Japan's imports from	
	1981	(%)	1981	(%)
USA	38,609	25.4	25,297	17.7
Saudi Arabia	5,876	3.9	21,482	15.0
Indonesia	4,123	2.7	13,305	9.3
Australia	4,779	3.1	7,419	5.2
China	5,095	3.4	5,292	3.7
United Arab Emirates	1,494	1.0	8,836	6.2
Korea, Rep. of	5,658	3.7	3,389	2.4
Germany, FR	5,968	3.9	2,429	1.7
Taiwan	5,405	3.6	2,523	1.8
Canada	3,399	2.2	4,464	3.1
UK	4,789	3.2	2,694	1.9
Singapore	4,468	2.9	1,944	1.4
Hong Kong	5,311	3.5	669	0.5
Malaysia	2,424	1.6	2,927	2.0
USSR	3,259	2.1	2,021	1.4
World, total	152,030	100.0	143,290	100.0

Source: Japan Tariff Association, *The Summary Report: Trade of Japan*, December 1981.

Note: * In order of total value of exports plus imports in 1981.

Deep down, too, Japan is fully aware that hawks in the West fear an economic or industrial Pearl Harbor sometime in the future if Japanese exports are allowed to flourish uncontrolled. It may sound irrational, but it helps explain why the Japanese desperately want to be loved and understood.

The West's protectionist tendencies have, to some extent, been side-stepped through a period of rapid direct investment by Japan in foreign countries. The rate of direct investment has doubled since the late 1970s, most notably through big projects in the advanced nations. By 1982 direct investment overseas was running at £5.5 billion and Japan had a total of £40 billion invested outside its shores,

Table 1.4 Exports and imports by commodity and country, 1980 (US$ million, customs clearance basis, exports, f.o.b., imports, c.i.f.)

		Foodstuffs (0, 1)*	Raw materials (2, 4)	Fuels (3)	Chemical products (5)	Machinery/ transportation equipment (7)	Other industrial products (6, 8)
Japan	Exports	1,589	1,580	523	6,619	75,780	42,012
	Imports	14,666	24,813	70,072	5,928	8,390	15,114
USA	Exports	30,318	25,688	8,017	22,430	82,810	38,854
	Imports	19,935	11,954	82,251	8,956	63,837	59,147
Germany, FR	Exports	9,241	4,797	7,278	24,318	85,414	57,191
	Imports	20,181	15,397	41,948	13,314	35,041	55,395
France	Exports	17,218	4,617	4,606	13,249	36,830	33,914
	Imports	12,566	8,731	35,857	12,169	28,814	35,696
UK	Exports	7,602	3,366	14,925	12,303	39,559	34,167
	Imports	14,345	8,940	16,039	7,310	30,301	39,484
Italy	Exports	5,286	1,422	4,410	5,505	25,254	35,112
	Imports	11,793	10,829	27,479	7,993	20,049	19,631

Source: OECD, Statistics of Foreign Trade.

Note: * Commodity categories in parentheses are based on Standard International Trade Category (SITC).

including £21 billion in America and £6.5 billion in Europe. It is a trend certain to continue.

By contrast, direct investment by Western and other foreign nations in Japan has been minuscule, totalling only £30 million by the end of 1982, or well under 10 per cent of the Japanese investment in their own countries.

The economic slow-down has come at a crucial time for Japan, which is facing increasing demands for welfare spending as its population grows old at a faster rate than in any other advanced industrial nation.

The postwar baby boom is currently producing a tidal wave of middle-aged Japanese, which by the late 1990s and beyond threatens to swamp the welfare system. Official Japanese estimates are that by the year 2000 some 15.6 per cent of its population will be 65 or over. Twenty years later, in 2020, the percentage will have climbed to 21.8 compared with only around 16 per cent of America's much larger population. It is also calculated that in France it has taken 175 years for the proportion of its population over 65 to rise from 5 to 12 per cent, and some 80 years in the case of Germany. In Japan the rise from 5 to 12 per cent is likely to be reached by 1990 – in only 40 years. As recently as 1980 the proportion of the Japanese population over 65 was 9 per cent, below America's 11 per cent.

Japan's long-term planners are worried about other population statistics. For example, eight people in work currently support each Japanese pensioner. But if present trends continue, each person aged over 65 will be supported by only three workers in the year 2020.

All this presents Japan's planners with a serious dilemma. On the one hand the government could continue the economic drive for growth and introduce measures such as greater work sharing to create employment and thus increased contributions to the exchequer. On the other hand those in work will have to make larger and larger contributions to the welfare system through higher taxes and social security payments.

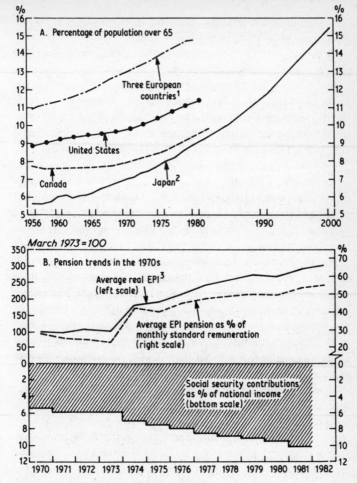

Figure 1.1 Ageing and pension trends

Sources: Economic Planning Agency, Ministry of Health and Welfare, OECD Secretariat.

Notes:
[1] France, Germany and United Kingdom.
[2] For 1985, 1990, 1995 and 2000, projections by the Ministry of Health and Welfare, November 1981 (medium variant).
[3] EPI: Employees' Pension Insurance, the general pension scheme for private firms.

All the indications are that the 1980s will see slower economic growth in Japan and therefore the likeliest prospect is that personal taxes will have to rise to accommodate the increased welfare spending.

At the same time, the government faces a serious problem in raising funds from the savings market to meet its share of the demand for rising welfare spending. The Japanese, once inveterate savers, are putting less away for a rainy day and economists reckon the savings trend is in long-term decline. Therefore if the government is to continue raising sizeable sums of money from security markets to fund increasing demands for welfare payments, the burden will have to fall on either the private taxpayer or private industry.

As a result the immediate oulook for the Japanese economy is not good. Low personal taxes and very high rates of research and investment spending by private industry provided much of the drive for Japan's 'economic miracle'. Workers saved, deposited money in the banks; the banks lent to industry and the government, which promptly re-invested in the future. Japan may have to come to terms with slow economic growth, rising personal taxes and sluggish capital investment. It will also have to learn to live with higher unemployment.

Slower growth alone will emphasize the point, but there is also a fear that many of the ageing or declining industries now in the MITI intensive care unit will prompt a further drop in the numbers employed in manufacturing industry. In the past, growing service industries, such as tourism and banking, have come to the rescue by providing many new opportunities. But they may not necessarily be able to take up sufficient of the slack while Japan waits for new jobs to be created by the massive programme to develop the electronics, biotechnology, aerospace and other new industries of the future.

Forecasts prepared by the government's Economic Planning Agency suggest that manufacturing industry's share of both output and employment will fall away by the turn of the century. Output is predicted to decline from 43.1 per cent of the economy in 1970 to 31.6 per cent in the year 2000, while the services sector, including transport, will have grown more rapidly from under 51 per cent in 1970 to 64.2 per cent by the turn of the century. Similarly the percentage of the workforce employed in manufacturing industry, including construction, will decline from over 35 per cent in 1970 to 33.3 per cent by the twenty-first century, and the services sector will have more than compensated by raising its proportion from just 47 per cent in 1970 to almost 62 per cent by the year 2000.

Unemployment, for the moment, remains a small problem in Japan, which is just as well since being out of work is particularly regarded as a social stigma. Current unemployment of under 2.5 per cent is modest compared with 13 per cent in Britain and 9.5 per cent in America. However, it is generally accepted that Japan's unemployment figures do not accurately reflect the true numbers of jobless, and the picture is further distorted by the fact that around 25 per cent of the working population is still engaged on a 'jobs-for-life' basis. Despite Japan's fiercely competitive trading environment, shedding labour does not occur as early or as frequently as those in the West might imagine.

Lifetime employment, which is mainly reserved only for those employed in the truly large companies, is probably one reason why Japan's trade unions appear, by European standards, docile and co-operative. Or, more realistically, it could be that there has been little mileage in militancy while the Japanese economy has been growing at breakneck speed and workers' wages have been advancing much faster than inflation. Significantly though, trade union membership in Japan has declined sharply in relation to the overall workforce, while strikes in industry are a rarity and the rate of absenteeism is very low.

It is an open question whether substantial change is looming on Japan's labour front. The wealth generated in the 1960s and 1970s has produced a workforce which increasingly demands more leisure and may even be chipping away at Japan's famous work ethic. Will the current crop of youngsters want to work six days a week for the same company for the rest of their lives, rarely taking their full holiday entitlement, and still salute the company flag every morning?

There will, unquestionably, be clashes between the young and old over the commitment of the individual to the ideals fashioned largely by the necessity of postwar rebuilding. The urgency which drove people in the 1950s may not seem quite so relevant in the 1990s.

However, Japan's in-built resilience, its ability to summon the huge resources of national consensus, and the experience gained from the first economic miracle all combine to suggest that, if any nation is to succeed in the coming decades, it will be Japan. Or, as one foreigner, resident in Tokyo for seven years, so aptly put it: 'The Japanese are the most aggressive people on earth. At the moment, they are channelling that aggression into trade and industry.'

Note on sources

The majority of the statistics given in this chapter were compiled from official Japanese sources. These included the Economic Planning Agency, the Ministry of Finance, the Ministry of International Trade and Industry, the Science and Technology Agency and the Ministry of Education. I am also grateful to trade unionists, bankers and economists who provided valuable help and assistance, but most of all I would like to thank the many Japanese people to whom I spoke. Further information on Japan can be obtained from the Japan Information Centre, 9 Grosvenor Square, London W1, and the Japan External Trade Organization, 19–25 Baker Street, London W1.

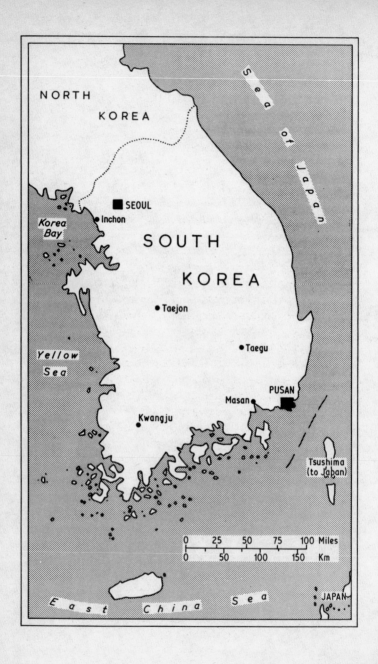

2 SOUTH KOREA

JANE McLOUGHLIN

It's natural, on first arriving in any foreign place – another country, another culture – to look first for signs of similarity with home. It's a jumping-off point for measuring the differences. What comes as a surprise, arriving at Seoul airport in the evening, is its lack of obvious foreignness.

Of course in daylight, and at closer scrutiny, you learn how different it is, but that first impression is astonishing. There are even London plane trees and European limes bordering some of the roads, and on the way into town the relentless traffic, the freeways, the mid-town multi-storey blocks were almost disappointingly familiar. Oddly, the strongest first impression of foreignness was the Musak in the bus which amid the din could have been Indian or Turkish but never, never American or European.

And all this is a surprise because I think most people visiting Korea for the first time would not be sure what to expect. Till well into this century, it was known to the world at large as the Hermit Kingdom; then we knew it as a country occupied by Japan, later torn apart by the Korean War. My geography books described it as mountainous, with very hard winters, a place where the bulk of the population lived off the land, growing rice in the flatlands which bound the rivers poking like spokes of a wheel into the mountainous mass from the coasts – population 40 million; area comparable to the British Isles.

The Koreans too must have to remind themselves how things looked before 1953, with before and after aerial photographs on the walls of the purpose-built offices in the new industrial towns, either in Seoul or the cities of the south-east which specialize, like enormous company towns, in a particular industry. These cities have claimed most of the workers now, who leave the old to tend the paddy fields while they seek higher wages or educational opportunities in the cities.

Perhaps Korea has been developed to look like any international big city to prove a point. Even the buildings are fiercely competitive – a new office block will be the tallest in Asia, new hotels will be the biggest and the best, new banks the glossiest – because Korea is going to be, is already on the way to being, a force in the world. Their national sporting symbol is the bow and arrow, and Koreans today see themselves as being like arrows fired from the past and now in flight towards the national target of an industrially developed, independent future.

If that's your goal, then even the recent past is not particularly promising: occupation by the Japanese, the war which split North and South and still shows the scars in the national obsession with infiltration from the North – fears fuelled by the destruction of the Korean airliner and the assassination in Rangoon in 1983 of many of the key men in the South Korean government. There are still 39,000 American troops providing a protective barrier for the South against attack from the North.

Then take a few more ingredients which made Korea a country of outsiders as far as the industrialized nations were concerned. Their language is akin to Finnish and Hungarian; their long-standing cultural tradition is Confucian. What they have done in the past thirty years is to preserve their uniqueness but spring into the second half of the twentieth century in one giant leap.

An everyday example: they went straight from the cash economy to credit cards, leaving out the whole system of cheque books. One English emigrant who has lived there for some years describes how, when he has to pay large bills, he stuffs his suitcase with *won* bills – at something like 1200 *won* to £1, *won* millionaires are common – and goes out and pays with notes. At least in Seoul, he would never be mugged.

But the ever-present sense of danger, the national defensiveness against their enemies, has provided a spur to develop a thrusting and fast-growing industrial programme, designed to create wealth as a source of power and independence, and through them, security.

Confucianism still pervades. You wonder, after a while, why all the cars on the teeming roads that aren't the bright little taxis are black. Most look like Ford Cortinas and Granadas too, but their colour is not the result of a joint industrial agreement on making cars between Ford and Hyundai; it's because Confucius taught that dark colours lend dignity. But I don't know whether the message in the lift at Hyundai, 'Credit is better than Gold', comes from Confucius, and they only laughed when I asked.

They laugh all the time. The Koreans are the jokers of the Pacific, and they play hard. But they earn their pleasures. Work and virtue are closely allied for them, and they have the work ethic like other people get the common cold. It is fired by the national belief that everyone each day must do his or her utmost, but the social structure also feeds the work ethic. The personal priority of each Korean worker is his or her country and family. The social welfare structure of the country depends on filial duty, which demands that a father support the sons through their thirties and forties until the eldest is able to look after the old father and mother in their retirement.

Acceptance of this apparently goes very deep – and undoubtedly saves the government an enormous amount in public spending. Of course the more educated and high-powered the son, the easier the retirement, but the head of a Korean corporation who has studied at Harvard Business School and travelled widely can still say with all sincerity: 'Truths change, but there is one truth that will never change, that you want your son to work hard and study and do well by working hard, and you will work to pay for that. That truth doesn't change, and in 100 years it will be the same.'

Even so, there are indications that after industrialization will follow the moral and philosophical trends we have seen in America and Europe. Already, first sons, who tradition-ally take on the burden of the parents, are finding it harder than their younger brothers to find wives. Also, the still-small voice of women demanding equality and committing themselves to a career, rather than simply working in a factory until they marry and have children, may play some part in changing the old order.

But now, everyone works for the good of the country. The Koreans are emotional people – after the bombing in Rangoon, they went about in the streets openly weeping, biting themselves and smeared with blood in their grief. But they spent no energy on public posturing internationally, expressing their outrage in still greater efforts at home. An official in the Ministry of Commerce and Industry said: 'The majority of the people concentrate their energy to work hard and develop industries since Rangoon. We have to make our power stronger to make the nation stronger.'

This shows at every level. On a Seoul back street, I saw a road cleaner climb one of the trees and shake down the loose leaves of autumn so that he could sweep them up meticulously; two men darted like fish through the eight-lane rush-hour traffic to wipe the road markings with washing-up liquid; in the tunnels under Seoul, which is where the shops you don't find fronting the streets huddle in hundreds of warm underground streets, women work endlessly cleaning the tiles, and chipping and replacing any that are broken.

It shows in the offices, where an Englishman helping to run a joint-venture merchant bank was astonished to find his typists sitting in their outdoor coats in the freezing office. He asked if the heating had failed, but was told no, they didn't turn it on to save fuel, and because they worked harder in the cold. This was the case too in the vast Hyundai car factory at Ulsan, in the south-east of the country, where men working an extra shift to meet the day's targets were doing so in temperatures not much above freezing in unheated buildings.

But we should be careful in making the easy European condemnation of 'slavery' and 'exploitation'. It is simple for us to put the furious growth and commercial competition of Korea down to exploitation of cheap labour and intolerable conditions. It is not seen like this by the workers themselves, but as a sacrifice they make for the country, and for their own eventual individual benefits through earning more. And of course from our Western viewpoint we answer, well, they would, wouldn't they, and we call the industrial and political ends which they serve a con. But put this to them, and they will laugh at our twisted Western sense of humour. They think our industrial set-up quite hilarious anyway, because they cannot identify with our goals.

Perhaps that has something to do with Confucius – but today the creed which is gaining ground is the nationalistic Chongdogya, though so also is Christiantiy. From whatever source, there is an enormous sense of pride and participation in the country's achievements.

When the Koreans talk about starting from scratch in the 1950s, they mean it literally. The North Koreans had razed Seoul, and penetrated all the way to Pusan before being driven back. The North Korean border is only about 32 kilometres from Seoul. Though the mountains which ring the city offer some protection, they also provide cover for infiltrators. So the South Koreans looked to the much more easily defended south-east of the country for sites for the

Table 2.1 General indicators of the fifth economic plan

	Unit	1980	1986	Average annual rate of increase (%) 1982–6
GNP:				
In 1980 prices	Trillion *won*	35.0	53.7	7.6
	US$ billion	57.4	90.0	7.6
Population	Million persons	38.1	41.8	1.6
Per capita GNP:				
In 1980 prices	Thousand *won*	919	1283	5.9
	US$	1506	2170	5.9
Increase in GNP deflator	%	27.7	9.5	10.8
Commodity exports (current prices)	US$ billion	17.2	53.0	11.4*
Commodity imports (current prices)	US$ billion	21.6	55.5	8.4*
Current account (current prices)	US$ billion	−5.3	−3.6	–

Source: Economic Planning Department, South Korea.

Note: * Rate of increase in real terms.

planned industrial development. There the rivers provide water and flat development land, and the coast makes it easy to transport steel from Pohang Steel to Ulsan car works or the huge shipbuilding yards, or chemicals to the textile industry. And behind this are the massive central mountains as a natural defence.

In 1984 Korea was mid-way through its fifth economic and social development plan. These five-year plans have been the basis of a revolution to transform the economy and the industrial base of the country – genuinely a Keystone Kops chase of an industrial revolution. Even as short a time ago as 1976, pictures of the sites of Changwon, the biggest of all these towns dedicated to specialist industrial production (in this case machine tools and heavy plant), show a few scattered dwellings round the paddy fields, and the slow river through their midst. Now, there's a series of purpose-built cities housing some half a million people each. They are all geared to serve the industries in which they specialize – Pusan for shipbuilding, Ulsan for cars, Yosu for petrochemicals, acrylic at Masan.

Changwon, for instance, houses over 100 different factories, all dedicated to machine tools and heavy plant. The city has grown around this, with huge blocks of apartments for the workers and their families, schools for the children and for specialist training in the technology of the industry; banks, hotels, hospitals, sports grounds, all provided by the companies ultimately for the companies.

The first four economic plans charted growth and industrial progress in terms of production figures and increased output. The fifth is crucial because it marks the transition from a rapidly developing but distinctly Third World economy to its consolidation as a newly developed economy.

The country has very little in the way of natural resources – no oil, no source of energy. Even its once tree-covered mountains were denuded by the Japanese for the war effort, and the Koreans are replanting now at the rate of 1 million a year. But Korea's development has been export-led, and one of the problems to come to terms with is keeping down production costs while at the same time improving quality to compete on international markets. Korea can no longer compete, for instance, with Taiwan's production costs, and the Koreans are looking over their shoulders at China as that country emerges to compete with them.

But first, what has been achieved already is remarkable. In 1961 Korea's per capita gross national product (GNP) was $82; in 1981 it was $1,640. The country spent $24.25 billion on imports in 1982; in 1984 Korea's growth rate was 8 per cent (higher than the 7.5 per cent projected in the fifth economic plan) and inflation, which ran at 44 per cent in 1979, was under 3 per cent. At the same time, the country's $42 billion

Table 2.2 Industrial origin of GNP (trillion won in 1980 prices)

	1980 (A)		1986 (B)		(B/A)	1982–6 Average annual rate of growth (%)
	Amount	Composition (%)	Amount	Composition (%)		
GNP	35.0	100.0	53.7	100.0	1.5	7.6
Agriculture, forestry and fisheries	5.9	16.9	8.0	14.8	1.3	2.6
Mining and manufacturing	10.7	30.7	18.7	35.0	1.7	10.8
Manufacturing	10.3	29.4	18.2	34.0	1.8	11.0
		(100.0)		(100.0)		
Light industry	4.8	(46.2)	7.9	(43.3)	1.6	9.5
Chemical industry	2.8	(27.4)	4.5	(24.8)	1.6	8.8
Metal industry	1.0	(9.7)	1.6	(9.0)	1.6	6.8
Machinery industry	1.7	(16.7)	4.2	(22.9)	2.4	17.6
SOC and other services	18.4	52.4	27.0	50.2	1.5	7.3
SOC	6.3	17.8	10.0	18.6	1.6	8.9
Other services	12.1	34.6	17.0	31.6	1.4	6.4

Source: As Table 2.1.

Table 2.3 Expenditure on GNP (trillion *won* in 1980 prices)

	1980		1986		1982–6 Average annual rate of increase (%)
	Amount	Composition (%)	Amount	Composition (%)*	
GNP	35.0	100.0	53.7	100.0	7.6
Consumption	27.6	78.8	36.7	70.4	5.3
Government	4.4	12.6	5.6	11.2	4.0
Private	23.2	66.2	31.1	59.2	5.5
Gross investment	10.9	31.0	18.0	32.4	8.8
Fixed capital formation	11.1	31.7	17.0	30.1	9.0
Increase in stocks	–0.2	–0.7	1.0	2.3	–
Total exports	13.7	39.0	26.3	46.8	10.9
Total imports (–)	17.1	48.8	27.4	49.6	7.9
Domestic savings	7.4	21.2	16.9	29.6	–
Foreign savings	3.4	9.8	1.1	2.8	–

Source: As Table 2.1.

Note: * Composition in current prices.

foreign debt is among the highest in the world, but there is no international concern at all about the country's ability to repay. Servicing this debt accounts for 15 per cent of GNP.

From the first economic plan in 1962, total GNP grew from $12.7 billion to $57.4 billion at 1980 prices. The value of exports increased from $50 million to $17.2 billion. Over the same period employment in agriculture, forestry and fisheries fell from 63.1 per cent to 34 per cent, while the mining and manufacturing sector grew from 8.7 per cent to 43.4 per cent. The number of people below the poverty line fell from 40.9 per cent to 12.3 per cent.

The current – fifth – economic plan stresses the importance to Korea's industrial future of energy prices. The plan, which applies until 1986, presupposes that the oil price rise per barrel will be from $30 in 1980 to $60 or even $70 in 1986.

Previous 'oil shocks' have already shown the dangers to Korea of inflation which leads to increased wage demands and higher production costs.

Table 2.4   Population and employment

	1980 (000s)	1986 (000s)	Average annual rate of increase (%)	
			77–81	82–6
Total population	38,124	41,839	1.55	1.55
Population 14 years old and over	25,335	29,312	2.8	2.5
Economically active population (labour force participation rate, %)	14,454 (57.1)	16,948 (57.8)	2.5	2.8
Employed population	13,706	16,268	2.3	3.0
Agriculture, forestry and fisheries (composition, %)	4,658 (34.0)	4,410 (27.1)	–3.6	–1.1
Mining and manufacturing (composition, %)	3,095 (22.6)	4,105 (25.2)	2.6	5.6
SOC and other services (composition, %)	5,952 (43.4)	7,753 (47.7)	8.3	4.4
Unemployed population unemployment rate (%)	749 5.2	680 4.0		

Source: As Table 2.1.

The average industrial wage is about $325 a month, and so far industrial expansion has not taken place because of domestic demand. It is exports and international competitiveness that the Koreans have been seeking.

This may be changing, partly because of the international recession. But still, a Korean wanting to buy an ordinary Hyundai Pony car will have to pay $4500, compared with an export price of $3000, and there are twenty-three separate domestic taxes on such a car to discourage the buyer. Partly, this is probably to discourage unnecessary use of energy; partly it may be because the government would rather the money was either saved or spent on the education of the future workforce.

But the fact remains that the 1978 oil shock in particular had an unforeseen effect on the Korean economy. The country had earned considerable convertible dollar currency by manning and carrying out construction contracts for the oil-rich nations of the Middle East. The government accepted the contract, paid the Korean workers in *won* and was itself paid in dollars. But when these construction contracts were cut back with the end of huge oil profits, the Korean government had to increase domestic building. This has led to a higher standard of living, and will continue to do so, but it has also brought a very stringent liquidity squeeze as cash flow problems grow. In the end, while companies have been able to produce better-than-expected financial results, this is often due to lower interest and inflation rates, and the squeeze has actually hit those at the end of the chain, the workers, which in turn may put off any immediate boom in domestic consumption. This perhaps provides an opening to talk about the role of government in both industrial planning and economic and social management.

The government of President Chun Doo Hwan was struck a heavy blow at Rangoon. Many of his best men, including the most experienced administrators, were killed. Some were old colleagues from his days in the armed forces; they tended to stand for an authoritarianism which was already becoming repressive in the universities. Restless students challenged the traditional Confucian reverence for the old, as the ever more highly educated young are bound to do.

There is an opposition party in Korea. It is said to be supported financially by the government, but it is more than a cipher. It acts as a brake, a force for discussion of issues, and a push, if not exactly a powerful one, towards liberalization. During 1984 the government eased considerably the restraints on free debate, particularly among students. At one stage, there were frequent incidents involving riot police on the campuses, and young people bitterly resented the number of plain-clothes agents who mingled with them to detect signs of dissidence. This year, the riot police have been taken off the campuses, and university students can demonstrate freely within the bounds of the universities.

Such steps towards democratization are also part of the new economic climate. Once stabilized, Korea's economy must settle down to live with its competitors, which will involve introducing free competition and the liberalization of protective restraints against competitors. This requires universities to provide personnel capable of achieving technological equality with competitors. Without giving autonomy to this vital section of society, the government is unlikely to be able to force Korea away from its old image as a producer of low-quality goods, cheap because of labour costs, towards status as a producer of high-quality products, competitive because they are produced by more technologically advanced methods.

That average monthly wage of $325 is invariably invested, once basic living costs are paid, in education. Korean primary schooling is free, but after that, education must be paid for and 80 per cent of Koreans spend twelve years in full-time education. The competition for university places is so intense that only one-sixth of all those who reach the standard win places. Nor does the thirst for more knowledge involve only an élite – Korea has a number of television learning programmes too, and it is quite usual for people to get up early and do 20 minutes English and perhaps a quarter of an hour French or Japanese with the television language service, which starts at 5.30 every morning.

One young Korean management trainee with one of the big corporations showed me his English class book. What happens is that the television shows old B-movies, and the student follows what is said from a book with the text in both Korean and English. 'It's good, because we also learn about European social life,' he said. It was a story about a young man in love with a girl who loves his best friend, expressed in dated colloquialisms, like 'old bean', but at 5.30 it's as compulsive viewing as anything could be.

But this young man's determination to do well for himself and his company was overriding. He had brothers and sisters, and felt an obligation to help his father pay for the best education possible – for sisters as well as brothers. They lived in Kwong-ju, several hours' train journey from the room he rented in Seoul, but he went home at weekends when he could. His working day started at 8.00 am, and he was at the office until 6.30 pm at least. In the evenings, he would meet a friend sometimes, and they would go to a film, or sit over a few beers and discuss what they should do to gain ground in their careers. He tried to explain what this meant to him. It had little to do with earning more – a pay rise pleased him not so much for what he could buy, but because it showed that he was pleasing those above him in the company. He felt a great sense of personal loyalty to the chairman, for whom he had deep respect. When it came down to it, he seemed to want status and respect from his peers much more than an improved standard of living. But he also wanted to get married. He had been writing to a girl he had met at university, who now worked as a statistical librarian in another town. He thought they were engaged, and hoped to marry her in 2 or 3 years. But she had met someone else. 'I am very sad. Last night I thought I would jump out of the window of my room, but this is not good for my family. Now I must find another wife.'

He was lucky, he said. He had his family. He spoke of over 1 million families in South Korea who have someone – a father, mother, brother or sister – lost to them in North Korea. He says he would like to come to Europe, to practise his English and French. He believes that Europe must be a wonderful place for a holiday, but he could see little point in working there as a part of developing his career. His view, and it was a common one, is that Western Europe is no longer significant as an industrial competitor; British shipbuilders can provide technological expertise, but in joint ventures in Korean yards they are not seen as rivals. West Germany too has steel technology to pass on, and machine-tool technology,

Table 2.5 Major social indicators

Indicators	Unit	1980	1986
Ratio of recipients of compulsory education at middle school	%	–	25.7
College enrolment ratio	%	15.8	31.2
Housing supply ratio	%	74.5	78.4
Average floor space per person			
Piped water supply ratio	%	55.0	70.0
Sewerage extension ratio	%	6.0	25.0
Subway utilization ratio	%	7.5	40.0
Telephone supply ratio (per 100 persons)	Unit	7.1	19.3
Population per physician	Person	1485	1275
Average daily calorie intake per adult	Calorie	2668	2816
Ratio of medical insurance coverage to total population	%	29.5	65.9
Ratio of industrial accident insurance coverage to economically active population	%	26.0	40.6
Income share of bottom 40% households	%	15.4*	17.5

Source: As Table 1.1.

Note: * 1978.

but Western Europe has declined 'from the higher cost of labour and harassment of working by strikes'. What will happen to Europe? 'We will come there on our holidays.'

That technology, though, still has a market value in Korea. They say they are pressing the Japanese for supremacy in all sorts of industries – steel, shipbuilding, textiles, electrical parts, even cars. But until recently, the Koreans have been dependent on what technological expertise the Japanese were prepared to provide. Now, the Koreans say, they have discovered that the Japanese are not originators of technological advances, so they are trying to set up joint ventures with technology-based firms in Europe and America.

The textile industry is a good example, and possibly the first to feel the draught of change. At the huge Hanil Synthetic Fibre Company at Masan, a director, Myong Sik Park, explained that his company is now being undercut by Taiwan and China:

> We want our own designs and we must develop the technology to improve the quality. Most of our machines are European, and we are improving the quality of our yarn with wool and cotton mix. We have sent our design experts to America for special education and in three to five years, we hope to produce not just from the samples of others, but to design our own styles for the international market.
>
> We no longer need to expand capacity. What we do need is to borrow to invest in new technology in our effort to increase quality.

It's a message reiterated from industry to industry. Although the heavy industries which are already seriously in decline in Europe – industries like steel, shipbuilding, machine tools and heavy plant – are still apparently profitable in Korea, and at least still have orders where even the Japanese are growing anxious about where new work will come from, the Koreans are well aware that to survive they must still export. And to export they must initiate technological advances rather than pick them up in the wake of the already developed industrial countries.

But they know that it will be some time before international protectionism decreases, particularly when they themselves want only to go through the motions of easing their own stringent protectionist measures against imports, partly because they have no wish thus to boost domestic spending. They would rather increase domestic saving, because investment money to spend on research and development and new technology is already at a premium.

In Korea, the kerb market is still a significant part of the funding scene for business. There was a kerb market scandal in 1983 which involved the government in considerable extra spending on support for businesses threatened after one of the street money-lenders, whose business is based on promissory notes, called in his notes when a number of customers could not meet these commitments.

Since then, the government has set about liberalizing the financial and banking sector – including changing its own role. Before, the government took a strong hand in allocating state loans, and in money made available from other countries in joint venture bank lending. Joint ventures in Korea entailed a compulsory government stake in the enterprise, which gave the government power to direct the spending of financial aid. This was part of industrial policy – or perhaps policing – to take the pressure off some and force an equitable distribution of work and markets. For instance, Hyundai Motors now makes very few of a commercial vehicle model it once produced in large numbers because the government wanted to prevent a failing rival from going out of business. And with the government intervening in who got loans, the vast bulk of available money in 1983 went to the country's 100 biggest companies, with a disastrous effect on smaller and medium-sized enterprises, who were forced to the kerb market for loans at huge interest rates.

The government has announced already its first proposals for cutting spending on internal investment: it will simply cut off funds to most state-run concerns, including the National Railroad, the Highway Corporation and the Citizens National Bank. The corporations will learn to survive through emphasizing efficiency and business management.

This is part of the fifth plan's commitment to bring principles of competition and the market mechanism to economic development with institutional reforms – and banking is a prime target.

In April 1984 the Finance Ministry announced that 'practically all restrictions imposed on foreign banks will be phased out for true national treatment'. This will not happen overnight, but it will mean that foreign banks will be able to raise funds more easily. They will also have to obey some restrictions placed on their Korean counterparts from which they were previously exempt. But at least, from early 1985, these overseas banks will have access to the Bank of Korea's rediscount facility for export-related finance, and by 1986 this will include import-related loans.

This liberalization marks a definite change from government policy in previous development plans. Korean industrialists, at all levels and in various manufacturing industries, are aware that they have to change their international 'image' as low-labour-cost producers of cheap, low-technology goods. This image is not totally deserved anyway – their huge success in producing ships, for instance, which has made them the world number two shipbuilder in a very short span of years (and they are now actually worrying the Japanese for the number one spot), was not achieved simply by overworking underpaid employees.

Before the first oil crisis in 1973–4, it was expected that there would be considerable demand in future for Very Large Crude Carriers (VLCCs) – ships of up to 1 million tonnes to transport crude oil around the world. There was considerable anxiety among the traditional shipbuilders of the world, in Europe particularly, because the new investment would have involved not only a technology making such ships prohibitively expensive, but also a liberalization of working practices tantamount to revolution, and politically unthinkable.

But the Koreans, who were starting more or less from scratch, created dry-dock facilities for building the giant ships, and on the vast sites of the yards they also built the capacity for making and fitting the entire ship. The expected demand for VLCCs did not materialize, and now may never do so. But the Korean shipyards are not idle. In Ulsan, a gallery of pictures cover the reception area of the shipyards showing the vast range of vessels the yard has built. There's no specialization here. Driving visitors around the working area, the car swoops down a ramp into the enormous dry docks planned for the VLCCs, and in the vast space they are building four oil tankers together, to use the space designed for the single giant. 'Mass-produced ships. You never thought you'd see that?' one of the workers joked. Few shipbuilding countries in the world, at a time of global recession, could fill their capacity with four ships at exactly the same stage of building, so that when the time came they could be given a group launching.

The men at the shipyard were worried about the recession, but they had two years' work in hand at least, and had diversified under the shipbuilding umbrella into building offshore oil platforms and other heavy-construction structures. The thousands of men from the Hyundai company hotel in Ulsan leaving their uniform modern blocks of apartments at 7.00 am and again at 8.00 am, swarming down the hill towards the shipyard to work, know they have a $4 billion-worth backlog of orders from America alone to keep them in work until 1985, and though new ship orders were sharply down in the first half of 1984 they seemed confident. South Korean yards won about 20 per cent of the world's new orders for ships in 1983, and can undercut even Japan on growing numbers of potential orders for vessels and offshore structures associated with the oil industry.

True, there is little scope for expansion of capacity – and the same goes for several of Korea's heavy industries, including construction, machine tools and textiles. The country already has capacity to spare, and the tendency to higher technology and better-quality output will not offer much chance of these industries' needs changing. But Koreans can face the facts of world recession and still maintain, and act upon, an apparently universal confidence in their own ability to overcome these facts of commercial life through their own efforts.

Table 2.6 Major planned projects to be finished by 1986 (US$ million in 1980 prices)

Projects	Con-struction period	Description	Capital required	
			Total	1982–6
Nuclear power plants (Woel Sung #2,5,6)	1976–85	3299 thous. kw	4052	1438
Expansion of shipyard	1982–86	4 million G/T–5.5 million G/T	879	879
New construction of shipyard	1983–85	0.5 million G/T	325	325
Expansion of passenger car capacity	1982–86	300 thous. units	1569	1569
Storage terminal for LNG	1981–86	3 million M/T	593	569
Storage terminal for LPG	1980–82	1 million M/T	107	51
Double lines of Honam railroad	1981–85	101.2 Km	213	200
East–West express way	1981–84	Taegu–Kwangju: 174.9 km	300	264
Subway of Seoul #2,3,4 and Pusan #1	1978–85	Seoul #2: 48.8 km Seoul #3,4: 57 km Pusan #1: 22.5 km	3441	2534
Choongju dam	1978–85	967 thous. m^3	487	362
Hapcheon dam	1982–86	4004 thous. m^3	167	167
Nakdong River estuary barrage	1982–86	1483 thous. km^3	110	110
Sewage treatment plant	1982–86	3857 thous. M/T/day	1074	1074
New Seoul agricultural wholesale market	1979–83	193 thous. m^2	116	93

Down the road towards Ulsan city centre from the shipyard, leaving the hotel to the left and the sea behind, there are several hundred yards of a continuous shed. It's a bit like giant undercover shelters for underground trains placed end to end at the terminus. This is Korea's answer to the criticism that its expansion plans for the steel industry look a little risky in view of the question mark which inevitably hangs over the future of the shipbuilding industry.

These huge sheds are intended to house the new motor manufacturing project which the Koreans claim will – with other industrial increases in output – increase demand for steel in line with growing output. These Ulsan sheds will house the production lines for thousands more Hyundai cars.

Incidentally, the question remains as to whether expansion of production can take up as much more steel as the Koreans plan to make. During 1985 the Pohang Iron and Steel Company (POSCO), which is state-owned, will start building a new $1.2 billion integrated steel mill at Kwangyang Bay, and this will be only the first of four to be built. The new mill, the first integrated mill in Korea, will increase POSCO's capacity by 2.7 million tonnes to 11.7 million a year.

The increased capacity is planned to meet growing domestic demand – and though construction at home is active now, this is partly to offset the very damaging effects socially and economically of the lack of work in the Middle East caused by the fluctuations of the oil industry. One area of real expansion, though, is in the car industry, and it is at Hyundai's Ulsan plant that an important project for a new export car model is under way. The company is one of the huge group of Hyundai concerns run by members of the Chung family, one of the best known of the *Dynasty*-style Korean families. Hyundai Motors is the concern of Chung Se Yung, who, like almost all top Korean businessmen, is highly educated and qualified, finished at Harvard Business school, and internationally respected in his field.

He is intensely proud of Hyundai's new F car, and of the way it will be produced. In conjunction with Mitsubishi (previous Hyundai models were made with a similar connection with Ford), the new car will be a 'family' model for export. The company is spending over £500 million to produce this car, which will be built in the huge new plant at Ulsan. This will have capacity for 300,000 units a year, though the present workforce of 11,000 will probably only grow by about 10 per cent to take on the additional production. This is an example of how many businesses in Korea are coping with the need for new technology while at the same time avoiding the social disasters of increasing unemployment by bringing it in: expand.

But that expansion brings us back again to the need for investment loans. Those car production lines are still in operation at 10.00 pm in the murky light and the considerable cold, each worker's concentration on the flashing display close to each line showing the shift's target car output, and the ever changing numbers of the finished models coming off the line. But the willing dedication of the workers, and even their ambition to earn more from these extra shifts, paid time and a half, is not enough in itself to raise Korea from the ranks of low labour cost/low-quality production to compete with Japan among the quality producers who still manage to keep their costs competitive internationally.

A considerable proportion of the money earned by those men in the half dark, though, will be spent on one of Korea's weapons – the education of the children who will make up the workforce. This country has a very highly educated and technologically trained workforce, and everyone – and that means everyone – is dedicated to learning more all the time.

So once the new technologies bought with the borrowed investment money are installed, Korean workforces are more than capable not only of using them to the full, but also of exploiting and improving them through their own skills. They look upon the Japanese as users of technology, not originators of it.

An official in the Ministry of Commerce and Industry, Un Suh Park:

Over the last 10 years, Korean firms liked Japanese technology, so the Japanese were our main investors. But now our manufacturers find the Japanese techniques originated in the US and Europe, so we now like to go there to introduce us to original technology. What we have to do now is develop our own technology, and this can be done through joint ventures.

The week President Reagan visited South Korea in November 1983, there were trade missions in Seoul from at least five different countries, to judge by the guest list at the international Hotel Lotte alone. America is Korea's biggest market abroad, taking nearly 30 per cent of its exports, while other south-east Asian countries took 18 per cent and Japan 25 per cent. As far as Europe is concerned, business with Korea is a question of trying to sell them technology and expertise, without having to buy back their products to compete with the home-produced European manufactured goods.

In fact, South Korea is looking to expand its markets not in Europe but in South America and in China. Expansion in China is greatly complicated by the relationship this huge potential market has with the North Koreans. Officially in the World Allegiance table, China and the USSR together support North Korea. But the relationship between China and Russia is not easy, and the Red Chinese have given some signals that they would like closer trading links with South Korea. In search of forging new trade relationships with any foreign country, and not just China, the government has eased restrictions on joint ventures, which are usually organized as licensing agreements between a Korean and a foreign company.

These licensing agreements can be restrictive to both sides – for example the licensing agreement with America in the defence field forbids the Koreans exporting arms anywhere else in the world, although this is a major industry.

But there can be advantages to both sides. One such joint venture is the Lucas CAV company set up at Changwon, which must be the fastest-expanding industrial park in the world, already a gigantic company town of half a million people. Lucas CAV is in a small modern factory which was flooded shortly before it was due to open. Within hours, volunteers had cleaned up and made everything ready for production to start on time – Lucas CAV was by then a Korean company and part of the patriotic surge to success. The company makes fuel-injection nozzles. There was one British manager there in 1984, though there had been more. Gradually the key roles, including managing director, were taken over by Koreans. The Koreans gained technological expertise and skill in making crucial parts, Lucas gained access to valuable markets in the Philippines, Taiwan and Malaysia. As well, Lucas found that in Changwon they used fewer people than in Britain to do the same job, and avoided restrictive demarcation over tasks.

These joint ventures have also been useful in mixing totally different business cultures, which will become ever more important as trade and manufacturing and marketing become more international.

Koreans do business after working hours, at Kaesaeng parties. Here business is never talked about, though it is the reason for the occasion. Local wine and spirits are served by the Korean equivalent of Japanese geisha girls, the Kaesaengs, dressed in their stiff silk national costumes, which fall like the long dresses of figures on playing cards and are in beautiful bright colours.

The point of these gatherings seems to be that those who watch each other look ridiculous can trust each other. They are very important as a way of subtly gaining or losing ground in business. The British perform very badly at Kaesaengs, because they are either hopelessly stiff and prim or drink too much to be able to score subtle points. For instance, one large British corporation thought that it had already won an order associated with the new underground system for Pusan. But then a high-ranking member of the Japanese government attended one of these knees-up with members of the Korean government, and found out beforehand that President Chun's favourite song was a number called 'Yellow shirts'. This he put his heart into singing, until the President, moved, thanked him and asked to do him a favour in return. 'The subway contract at Pusan.' And how could he refuse? The British in Seoul were also made very aware of the importance of the Kaesaeng, if they had ever doubted it, when a member of the last Labour government offended the Koreans quite seriously by refusing to take part in the ceremonial entertainments. Not that the offence was taken visibly, for the Koreans would think it rude to react. They are an enormously polite and punctilious people, and it can be insulting to them to forget to offer a business card or to seem less than respectful of someone's status.

The concept of respect for status is central to Korea, both internationally and at a domestic social level. The social order in Korea depends heavily on respect for elders. This applies in government and in the family. An old father kept by his eldest son and looked after by his daughter-in-law takes totally for granted that his views will not only be sought, but that he will dominate his son and his son's family while he lives. Age is the sum of knowledge, and Korea listens to its old men.

But, inevitably, this is changing, because the old men have no knowledge or experience of the world their children live in. The successful transition from old to new is at the heart of Korea's task for the medium-term future.

Any transition would probably be successful because the country is united by the single, central purpose of putting Korea on its own feet, of becoming a force in the world. This unity is fuelled by the sense of danger from North Korea, an implacable enemy whose hostility is constantly brought home to every South Korean. They accept, for instance, that only a very few of them should travel abroad, and then only when necessary, because of the danger of their passports being stolen and used by North Koreans to infiltrate the South. One chink in their enmity may be the need for South Korea to develop export markets in China, which is allied, along with Russia, on the side of North Korea, while America supports the South.

National feeling is fostered – in the offices the staff have a session of physical jerks at 4.00 pm, to help restore their circulation, and then at 5.00 pm they stand for the national anthem (an attempt was made to stop the roar of 11 million vehicles in Seoul for the anthem at 5.00 pm every day, but in the event it just wasn't feasible).

These are not, though, the robot-like figures we tend to think populate the industrial nations of the Pacific rim. They work harder than we do, but they are very highly motivated to do so, both personally and nationally. They play hard too; they have great thirst for life and experience. Nor are they ambitious in the grasping, devil-take-the-hindmost way of the Western company man. Perhaps it has something to do with their sense of humour: 'You think those mountains are beautiful; we wish they were not there so there could be flat land where we can cultivate,' said one, smiling.

For the Koreans have a long cultural tradition of their own; they are fine musicians and dancers. The sight of their new industrial cities sets European aesthetic nerves protesting, but in Korea the functional is good, not the beautiful. On with the new, off with the old, they proclaim. It's only history in the making. They have a lot of catching up to do. If the Koreans are like arrows, they are in flight from the ancient past to the future, and the present is being over-flown.

Note on sources

Apart from personal observation, sources included the fifth 'Five-Year Economic and Social Development Plan' of the South Korean Economic Planning Board; literature and information from the Korea desk of the British Overseas Trade Board, and 'Basic Foreign Investment Policy and Guidelines' prepared by the Foreign Investment Promotion Division of the Ministry of Finance in Seoul.

In addition, I spoke to civil servants in the Department of Economic Planning in Seoul, and the Finance Department. Also, at the British Embassy in Seoul, to the British Ambassador, and commercial and technical officials; to British bankers in Seoul involved in joint venture financing; to Shung Se Yung, President of Hyundai Motors.

In Pusan, Masan, Ulsan and Changwon I spoke to managers of steel, textile and motor manufacturers, and shipbuilders and machine tool makers, including the Korean and British joint management of the Lucas CAV project at Changwon. Mr Kim Lee of the Korean Embassy in London was also very helpful.

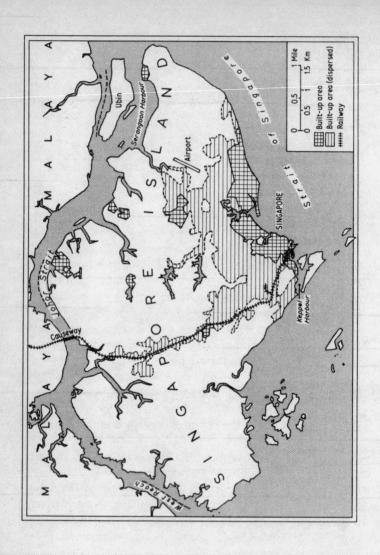

3 *SINGAPORE*

PETER LARGE

Singapore holds the richest asset for success in the post-industrial world – the asset of having nothing: no long-standing heavy industry to deaden its itch for change; no rich raw-material resources, like North Sea oil, to provide a treacherous cushion. Singapore's only exports that spring from its natural resources are goldfish and orchids.

Therefore it depends starkly for the 1990s and beyond on what the Singapore Establishment calls the 'brain indus-tries' – on how its 2.5 million people, uncrammed on an island smaller than the Isle of Man, succeed in selling their skills and services to the rest of their region and then to the world.

Therefore, too, Singapore is investing massively in higher education. Already nearly 10 per cent of school-leavers go to university. That proportion, reached within two decades, is marginally higher than Britain's, but Japan has already reached the 40 per cent level and Taiwan has passed 20 per cent. In 1983 Singapore produced as many computer science and electronics graduates, pro rata, as Britain did, and the numbers are climbing year by year. For those young people who do not make it to university, there is an even faster expansion in technical training.

As a result, there are young Singaporeans, born when it

was still predominantly a land of the poor, who today are entering their first jobs in a transformed nation whose per capita income is exceeded in Asia only by Japan's.

For these reasons academic futurologists love Singapore. It is the case study of their dreams: a garden-city state with a government that, even more than Japan's, has long preached – and is now proving – the 'information society' message that wealth must increasingly come from the skills and knowledge of a highly educated populace; that selling knowledge is becoming more profitable than making things; that greater wealth can be produced from the work of fewer but much more highly skilled people.

The theory behind the so-called 'sunrise industries' of information technology is now widely accepted by the governments of industrialized nations. The difference in Singapore, as it now joins that rich segment of the world, is that its politicians have for years talked openly – even evangelically – about it. In the West with its tradition of mass employment in initiativeless clusters, a tradition born of the first industrial revolution, politicians have been nervous about facing publicly the widespread and rapid change required in the new industrial revolution.

That post-industrial revolution is rooted in an axiom that has been obvious for millenniums: information is wealth, and rapid and wide access to information is power. Rulers survived by that principle long before Francis Bacon defined it in 1597. Through the centuries since then, man's methods of collecting, analysing and distributing information have been steadily refined. The big leap came with the building of the first bulky electronic computers at the end of World War II, though few people recognized the significance at the time.

The invention of the microchip, shrinking the computer to microscopic size, has finally brought that ancient truism to total realization. It has brought such a vast expansion of capacity, flexibility and speed in the handling of information that information itself is becoming the key economic resource, the top factor of production – more important than capital, labour, land or raw materials. And the clumsy label 'information technology' has won acceptance as the family title for all the tools of this new industrial revolution – a range that spreads down from communications satellites and cable networks through factory robots and office computers to the domestic television set.

Some of the keenest examples of the way in which the computer has freed information, allowing it to play its proper role, are to be found in the old realm of making things. Firms that have introduced true automation to their factories, linking automated production lines and warehouses in a computer information network, and thereby removing the need for mountains of paper records, have found that the key benefit is not saving on personnel or even raising quality. It is information. The manager of the paperless factory saves time, and therefore saves on expensive storing of parts, because at long last he actually knows what is happening, as it happens, rather than learning too late from paper score sheets.

But enough of theory. Let's move on to the ways in which Singapore is applying the theory. First, the root facts:

The republic of Singapore, just north of the Equator, is wedged between Indonesia and the tip of the Malaysian peninsula. Its population of 2.5 million lives on an island only 42 kilometres by 22. Singapore city itself is on the island's southern coast. The total land area, including 54 tiny islets, is 618 square kilometres.

Its place in world history began in 1819 when Sir Stamford Raffles established a trading station there. It was a British colony under various combinations of Indian, Malaysian and Colonial Office control until the Japanese occupation in 1942. Immediately after the war it was made a separate crown colony. The state of Singapore was pronounced in 1958 and the first general elections were held in the following year. Lee Kuan Yew has been prime minister and virtual ruler ever since; but Singapore's transformation into Asia's Commonwealth nation of the rich only truly began with the final divorce from Malaysia in 1965.

The island has no natural resources apart from its agricultural land (14 per cent). It has to import most of its food and all its energy from its less developed neighbours – and it has twisted that to temporary advantage by becoming a major oil-refiner. Even its water has to be piped from Malaysia, on a 1-kilometre causeway that also carries a road and railway across the Strait of Johore.

Its only resource, therefore, is the talents of its people. Some 77 per cent are Chinese (and they dominate the power centres to an even greater degree than that), 15 per cent are Malays (who mainly fill prole roles), and 6 per cent come from India, Pakistan and Sri Lanka.

The gross national product (GNP) was approaching £4000 a head in 1983. The economy grew by 10 per cent a year from 1978 to 1982 and still grew by 6.3 per cent in mid-slump 1982, then by 7.9 per cent in 1983. More than 70 per cent of GNP already comes from the service sector. Average weekly earnings rose 15.3 per cent in 1982 and by 9 per cent more in 1983 – and that in a country which has an inflation norm of around 1 per cent and an unemployment norm of under 3 per cent. Inflation did spurt to 11 per cent in 1982, under the pressure of rising import prices and what will probably be the last for some time of the big, government-orchestrated, annual pay rises. But it went back to normal again within a year.

Government spending goes on rising – 29 per cent more in 1982, 18 per cent more in 1983 – much of it going into long-term projects that strengthen the nation's infrastructure and boost the economy all round. And the balance of payments stays in the black. Another significant plus-point for the future is that 40 per cent of the population is less than 19 years old.

In foreign policy, Singapore has to tread a tricky path. Its basically neutralist stance has to take note of the economy's reliance on Western investment. Equally, it has to try to

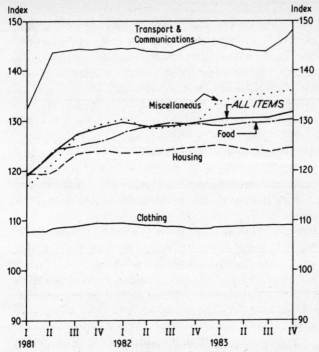

Figure 3.1 Consumer price index (June 1977–May 1978 = 100)

maintain accord with its much more populous – and much less prosperous – neighbours. It is a member of ASEAN (the Association of South-East Asian Nations), a pro-Western economic alliance formed in 1967. Of the other members – Brunei, Indonesia, Malaysia, Thailand and the Philippines – only Brunei holds comparable wealth. A parallel problem is that the populations of its closest neighbours, Malaysia and Indonesia, are mainly Muslim. The government has devoted great attention to building and maintaining an independent defence capability, based on compulsory national service and home-grown industries in small arms and aircraft maintenance.

Two relics of the colonial days have helped Singapore in its climb. One is the international language of English. Although only 12 per cent of children enter school already knowing English, they all have to learn it before they can win in the highly competitive, English-based education system, with British-pattern exams. The government has made English the one universal local language as well as the business language.

The other historical advantage, stemming from Singapore's pivotal position in south-east Asia, is the inherited – but modernized – docks business. The free port is second only to Rotterdam in turnover. Tankers and container ships queue along the coast and the port authorities claim that a ship leaves or enters port every 10 minutes.

But the real clue to Singapore's success has been a brave, consistent, government-generated, long-term industrial strategy. Professor Tom Stonier, head of the School of Science and Society at Bradford University, and one of the futurologists who has used Singapore as an example of a prospective post-industrial success, has made the point succinctly: 'To claim that most of this dramatic growth reflected inputs of capital is like saying that Einstein created the theory of relativity because he ate a good breakfast.'

Professor Stonier sees that strategy as having worked in two phases. In the early 1960s the emphasis was on import substitution. The government used high-tariff protection to help industries that would reduce the dependence on imports. In the second phase the emphasis shifted to export-orientated manufacturing. But that required foreign capital and technology, and so the Singapore Economic Development Board, formed in 1961, began to woo the big multinational companies with investment incentives.

The result was that by 1980 Singapore had 3300 manufacturing firms, employing 287,000 people, compared with 1000 firms employing 47,000 in 1965. But over the next two years it was the more traditional manufacturing industry that took the brunt of the slump, slowing Singapore's advance. This may have been a blessing in disguise, for the wealth is there to build the next stage, what Singaporean ministers call their 'second industrial revolution', advancing from labour-intensive industries into the knowledge-intensive industries of high technology and business services. That also involves an increasing emphasis on tourism as well as on a financial-centre challenge to Hong Kong.

A major part of that long-term strategy has been to raise wage levels, with the joint aim of encouraging people to acquire higher skills for higher pay and encouraging firms to automate production rather than use unskilled labour. This pay-boosting policy, run by a National Wages Council, has been incorporated in the government's ten-year Economic Development Plan. The methods and levels of pay settlements indicate how that plan is being fine-tuned as it unfolds.

Average weekly earnings rose 14 per cent in 1981 and 15.3 in 1982. But in 1983 – when inflation had been restored to a mere 1.2 per cent – the rise was held back to 9 per cent and back again to 5.7 per cent in 1984. Until 1983 the deliberations of the National Wages Council were firmly orchestrated by the government. Since 1983 – formally at least – that has not been so. The Ministry of Trade and Industry said the new arrangement was 'intended to eventually pave the way for direct wage negotiations between unions and employers'. The government's aim, in fact, is to shift union organization – and welfare backing – from an industry to a company base, a pattern that better suits the more fragmented new industries of information technology.

In the 1970s and early 1980s, as the population continued to grow by about 1.2 per cent a year, the workforce was boosted by university- and school-leavers who were born in the postwar baby boom. But such has been the rate of economic expansion that even in the recession unemployment remained low. The percentages were 2.9 in 1981, 2.6 in 1982 and 3.2 in 1983.

While dully listing those impressive statistics in its 1983 economic survey, the Ministry of Trade and Industry allows a glimmer of the arrogance of the new Singapore to slip through. In describing how more women have been able to return to work post-slump (45.7 per cent of women are at work), it gives as one of the causes 'the availability of foreign domestic help', which is mostly Malay and Filipino.

Another strand of government strategy is massive, sometimes high-risk, public investment in the infrastructure. The initial example was housing. Today 70 per cent of Singaporeans live in state housing, mostly high-rise flats, but flats with little trace of incipient grot. Most are surrounded by parklands and include meeting circles for the old and playgrounds for the children.

Other examples are Singapore Airlines' £1 billion investment in the latest wide-bodied jets; the start of work on a £1.5 billion rapid-transit rail network; more ritual days of tree-planting by the thousands to preserve the image of a city in a garden; the opening of the glittering new Changa Airport, which contains a virtual community of high-tech shops and Chinese restaurants; the rapid modernization of telecommunications; and another surge in hotel building despite the drop in occupancy during the slump. In fact, tower-block offices and hotels are replacing the slums of Chinatown at a rate that is causing the tourist industry anxiety about the exotica quotient. The skyscrapers press down on the old waterfront streets like an invading army of Goliaths.

The listing of those brave, brash developments provides a reminder that we have not yet examined the social discipline that underpins them. Singapore is moving to a tune that – so far, anyway – bears no remote resemblance to the post-industrial dream of an individual-enterprise world, involving a weakening in the levers of mass control and an increase in small, profit-sharing enterprises. Therefore, before we speed on to what the republic is actually developing in the 'sunrise' industries, it would be wise to take a look at the political background.

Singapore is a highly disciplined society – a bewildering blend of one-party state socialism with free voting and vigorously competitive capitalism. That can be partly ascribed to the Chinese character but the main cause is its political history. Dr Bob Taylor, an American historian who is a south-east Asia specialist at the London University School of Oriental and African Studies, says the key was the Chinese business community's backing of Lee Kuan Yew to subdue the crypto-Communists. The resultant political machine aimed to make the workers happy.

The outcome is a Commonwealth nation in which parliament meets occasionally; in which the People's Action Party monopolizes elections; in which television is censored; in which the newspapers are state-guided and are full of worthy propaganda about productivity and computer-training; in which any corruption is savaged; in which strikes are a rare sensation; and in which family-planning campaigns are openly aimed at raising the quality of the breeding stock.

In short, social engineering has become a way of life. But that discipline has brought economic prosperity to a much wider range of Singaporeans and has created a nation in which the slums have been replaced by estates set in parks and in which the new skyscraper city itself is full of greenery and glitter-clean (compared, say, with London or New York). The discipline is boosted by a bureaucracy which only hinders where it is designed to hinder – key projects are often completed months ahead of schedule.

The symptoms on the surface include fines of 500 Singapore dollars (around £150) for jay-walking, littering the streets or smoking in public places. Tipping is theoretically banned, and the Ministry of Culture's guide to visitors warns: 'Long hair is officially discouraged. Male visitors are advised to have their hair trimmed if it reaches the top of their shirt collar.' More significantly, there is little open debate about future directions. Press and television report ministerial pronouncements *ad nauseam* and with little counter-opinion or critical analysis. In the autumn of 1984 Dr Toh Chin Chye, former health minister and one of the ruling party's founder members now out of favour, said that Singapore was being cowed by the system. People were worried, he said, that if they spoke up they would be victimized. 'They are seeing shadows under every bush and that, I believe, is not good for Singapore.'

His surprising statement followed the announcement by Lee Kuan Yew that he plans to retire in 1988 after his 65th birthday. By then Mr Lee will have been prime minister for nearly thirty years, and there have been hints that his aim after that will be to become an elected president with power over the government's use of Singapore's financial reserves.

The old guard of the People's Action Party, who have helped Mr Lee to build the new Singapore, are beginning to fade away. Since the beginning of the 1980s a group of eight younger leaders has slowly emerged in the cabinet and the party's central committee. In 1984 Mr Lee promulgated a new series of policy initiatives which indicated that he wants a structure for the future not only in place but tested before he goes.

The announcements included another attempt to push the nation's gene pool up-market by re-emphasizing the birth-control incentives offered by the government, in order to change what Mr Lee calls the 'lop-sided pattern of pro-creation'; proposals to establish a sort of compulsory opposition; and the merger of the two main newspaper groups. This last was presented as a purely economic measure but journalists, nevertheless, indulged in that Singapore rarity, a protest demonstration.

The parliament does have two opposition MPs, one through a by-election in 1981, the other elected in the full parliamentary elections of December 1984. The new plan for a statutory opposition is to appoint – not elect – up to six non-constituency members, who will not be allowed to vote on key issues.

In a speech to parliament in August 1984, Mr Lee explained

his thinking bluntly. One-man, one-vote democracy had difficulty working anywhere, he said. It rarely worked in Asia and might not be best for Singapore. In the election four months later, Mr Lee's party took only 63 per cent of the votes, compared with 76 per cent in 1980.

On the genetic front. Mr Lee has urged young Singaporean career women – of whom there are many – not to put jobs before motherhood, and to marry men of their own intellectual standing in order to maintain the quality of the stock. The government has offered financial incentives to lower-income mothers to be sterilized – while giving educational priorities to the children of mothers with university degrees.

The non-graduate population is directed to follow a 'two is enough' family policy, but the sterilization campaign is not succeeding. The annual report of the Family Planning and Population Board shows that 6011 female sterilizations were performed in 1982 – a drop of 5 per cent. Male vasectomies increased by 8 per cent to 494. But the total of legalized abortions was 15,548, a 1.8 per cent rise. The average age of the women involved was 28.

Despite all that evidence, Professor Stonier, the futurologist from Bradford University, is convinced that the transformation into a graduate-crammed society is bound to democratize Singapore, and that point has also been made by the International Chamber of Commerce, which represents foreign firms in Singapore. Professor Stonier says that, whoever succeeds Lee Kuan Yew, the new generation will not accept the rigid controls of the present.

The negative evidence to support him is already emerging. Crime is rising, and video piracy is rife because of the television censorship. Ministers have repeatedly insisted that censorship must be continued to keep out the worst of Western values.

Prosperity has brought a drift away from traditional Chinese family responsibility towards selfish materialism. Therefore, the government has reintroduced religion into the secondary schools with an emphasis on Confucianism. Touchiness about the language issue is also a straw in the wind. Apart from the dialects, there are four official languages: English, Mandarin, Malay and Tamil. In 1983, as part of the government's educational drive in English, the National University of Singapore relaxed its second-language requirements.

Mr Goh Chok Tong, deputy prime minister and one of the leaders of the new guard, felt it necessary to explain that this should not be seen as a signal that the Mandarin mother tongue could be neglected. It would be a sad day, he said, when parents, teachers and students misread the signs in that way. He repeated a constant ministerial theme: 'We cannot be a rootless, deculturalized Westernized country, drifting in Asian waters.'

Another sign of the times was a 1983 survey which showed that 91 per cent of Singaporeans want to be consulted about any government decision affecting their lives. Mr Lee's social engineering is also beginning to encounter trade union opposition. Some of the older-industry unions, closely linked to government, are getting restive about the government's attempts to shift union organization from an industry to a company base.

Mr Lee, who was a union legal adviser in the colonial days of his youth, has ensured that the unions are involved in government policy and intertwined in the government machine. Some leaders of the Singapore National Trade Union Congress have been ministers at the same time. (Another oddity of the trade union world in Singapore is that some unions go into business as well; one runs a taxi combine.)

The changes required by the new industries of information technology are causing problems with pay as well as with union reorganization. For instance, Singapore Airlines has an ever increasing demand for computer specialists who – as in every other nation – are in short supply. In July 1983, therefore, it introduced a 'market comparison allowance', giving computer people 10 per cent more money than their fellows. The Air Transport Executive Staff Union objected because of the 'adverse morale factor' on other airline executives who are in the same salary structure.

A good example of the changes being wrought by the new high-tech businesses is to be found in Ang Mo Kio new town, in the centre of the island, north of Singapore city. There, set amid parklands and workers' flats, is a spotless, spacious factory that employs fewer than 300 people. But about a third of them have degrees in electronics and the rest all have several O-levels at least. They make nothing; they add expert value to the labour of others.

That factory encapsulates the aims of the new Singapore. And the factory's address encapsulates the disciplined way Singapore goes about it: Block 5002, Avenue 5, Industrial Park 2. The factory provides the brains – the microchip-crowded boards – for desk-top personal computers sold worldwide by the Californian-based company Apple. It takes the output of sub-contractors elsewhere in Singapore, whose employees do the soul-destroying job of placing all the fiddly bits into those boards. All Block 5002 does is test them and ship them.

But to do that, Apple's Singapore team has written its own computer software and has invented ways of improving the standard testing equipment imported from America. Mr Ron Pasari, the plant manager, who arrived in Singapore from Bombay via California, says that that value-adding innovation was achieved within two years. The only foreigners involved were Mr Pasari himself and two other computer scientists from California.

Block 5002 is also giving Singapore experience of the frenetic competition in information technology. Apple cut back on staff in the summer of 1983 because of the growing international price war in microcomputers – a development which produced a soothing statement by Mr Hwang Peng Yuan, chairman of the Economic Development Board, soothingly reported in the press. Mr Hwang explained the inevitable volatility of these new industries and emphasized the fact that because of the skills they had learnt, redundant staff had no trouble in finding jobs in other information-technology enterprises in Singapore. The board would therefore continue to court computer firms, he said, even if there was a likelihood of some firms closing down.

In any event, making microcomputers is only a secondary flow in the high-tech tide. Many industrialized nations now see the need to take a strategic hold on the high-cost, high-risk business of manufacturing the microchips themselves, rather than merely assembling them into products. These microscopic machines, carved into fragile fragments of silicon, are the 1980s equivalent of the nuts and bolts of the first industrial revolution – crucial to all industry. Therefore the Economic Development Board has worked hard to entice the chip-makers to Singapore. Two chip-making plants were being established in 1984, one by the leading American firm Texas Instruments, the other by a fast-growing Italian group, SGS. Another joint venture is intended to produce Asia's first top computer outside Japan, and there is now a whole cluster of industry making electronic components, computer disk drives, computer printers, and the like, predominantly for export.

The foundation for that expansion was laid between 1968 and 1981. In 1968 there were only five electronics factories, employing 700 people and with each worker producing value-added wealth of only 2000 Singapore dollars. By 1981 there were 182 factories, employing 68,000, with a value-added rate of 26,250 dollars per worker. The most illuminating figures there, of course, are the huge rises in value-added, reflecting the rise in the skills involved in the work.

The 1983–4 budget encouraged the industry further by making computers and office equipment eligible for a 100 per cent depreciation allowance in their first year. The government also offers grants to firms to encourage auto-mation and research and development (R & D). By 1983 more than 170 establishments were undertaking R & D. The projects included educational and industrial robots, pocket radio-telephones and automation machinery for the computer industry. State investment is also going into a science and technology park at the National University. Among the first tenants there are robotics and microcomputer firms.

The government's encouragement of automation meant that in 1983 the manufacturing workforce declined further, by 6 per cent – while productivity rose by 9 per cent. By 1984 there were more than 700 robots employed. That may seem an unstartling number, particularly since that government statistic includes those primitive hands (called pick-and-place units) which humbly move components from place to place and are not strictly robots at all. But the robot is an overblown symbol of industrial automation. The annual survey made – on the strictest criteria – by the British Robot Association shows that there were only 37,000 industrial robots at work worldwide by the end of 1983 (the British total was 1753).

A more significant measure of the rapid change in Singapore's factories is the calculation that between 1979 and 1984 the number of computer-run machine tools increased tenfold to a total of more than 500.

That modernization, however, is merely the means to the end. Computers and their allied machinery are only the tools to accelerate and broaden the handling of information, which is the ultimate key to future wealth. Mr Philip Yeo, chairman of the Singapore National Computer Board, says: 'Undoubtedly, Singapore will increasingly look towards information, after the human element, as the country's most precious resource. Likewise, organizations will come to grips with information as a factor of production and a corporate resource.'

Therefore the government is also encouraging the wider aspects of a service-based, information-based economy. The 1983–4 budget gave a five-year tax holiday on income earned from loans syndicated in Singapore, to help the banks in their competition with the rival city-state of Hong Kong to become established as the financial pivot of the region. (Professor Stonier has theorized that Singapore and Hong Kong might rival London and New York in future as business capitals of the world.)

Financial and business services contributed 34 per cent to the overall expansion of the economy in 1983, while manufacturing contributed only 5 per cent. In meeting the communications needs of the financial community, Singapore boasts that it has the highest density of telex machines in the world – 12,800 subscribers in 1983, with demand growing at more than 20 per cent a year. The microchip-managed successor to telex, which operates thirty times faster and prints its messages in letter quality, is now being introduced.

This brings us to another central element in Singapore's transition to a post-industrial economy: telecommunications. Everywhere the state of play in modernizing telecommunications provides a clue to a nation's ambitions. The emergence of one ubiquitous information-technology industry springs from the microchip-driven convergence of computing and telecommunications. The wider capability that microelectronics has brought to the collection and analysis of information loses much of its point if you cannot also distribute that information quickly. In Singapore's case that obvious need is given greater urgency by the city's role as a financial centre.

Singapore already scores well on the telecommunications test. The phone population passed 35 per 100 people in 1983. That is well below the British proportion, but it's high in Asian terms – and all the phones are now push-button. Investment in telecommunications was budgeted at more than £200 million a year throughout the mid-1980s. Proportionately, that is four times bigger than Britain's commitment.

What's more, in contrast to the British experience, the modernization of telecommunications is seen by the government as a central part of the strategic investment in

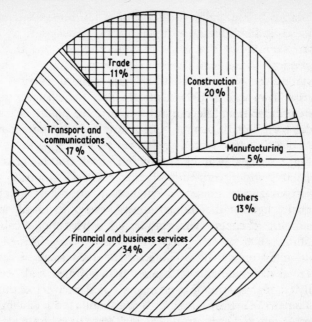

Figure 3.2 Contribution to real growth in gross domestic product by industry, 1983

the infrastructure of the economy rather than as a profit-maker in itself. Charges for international calls were reduced five times between 1979 and 1983. Mr Frank Y. C. Yung, chairman of the Telecommunications Authority, which also incorporates the old Post Office, actually reported 'satisfaction' at a fall in net revenue in 1982. He was pleased that the 'more daring approach' to investment had combined with the cuts in tariffs to produce lower profits, despite the continued expansion in the business.

That investment embraces new submarine cables, microwave links, satellite earth stations, computer-run phone exchanges, and optical fibre cabling. The overall purpose, as in all nations, is to transform the telecommunications network from the old analog (wave) form of handling the messages to the digital form of billions of bits of separate information in which the digital computer deals.

An example of the scope of this change is the British invention of optical fibres. Singapore claims to have installed the world's first fibre-optic cable to carry 'live' traffic. That was in 1977. Optical fibres (which have uses much wider than telecommunications) use pulses of laser light, travelling through minute strands of ultra-pure glass, to replace electricity and copper cables.

Light signals beat electricity on most counts: greater capacity, wider versatility, firmer accuracy (there is no electromagnetic noise to corrupt a message), greater security against the industrial spy, easier to install and becoming cheaper. The standard electric phone cable, holding 4800 pairs of copper wires, is arm-thick. The equivalent optical fibre cable (at the 1984 stage of commercial development) is thinner than a finger and needs only eight glass strands to do nearly twice the work of those 4800 pairs of wires. The strands are about a tenth of a millimetre wide and each strand carries 140 million bits of information a second. Fibre-optic transmission is digital; therefore it mates naturally with computer operations.

Strategic planning papers of the Singapore Telecommunications Authority, dealing with the futurological theme of the 'wired city', talk of using optical fibres to bring to the home a plethora of new services that 'can change the entire fabric of society'. They mention video phones, personal computers and multi-channel two-way TV being used over one multi-purpose optical fibre network to enable people to work and learn at home as well as to shop and bank from the home TV screen.

All that, of course, is standard stuff; and in terms of today's home use of such emerging services, Singapore is years behind Britain, France and Germany, let alone Japan and the United States. But Singapore's track record of change is such that a further transformation over the next decade is easy to envisage. In this case, the island's tight geography suits the purpose, and the accepted assumptions of social engineering are there to drive it. A report by the Telecommunications Authority's corporate planning team mentions 'much co-ordinated and far-sighted planning during the transitional period'.

Unsurprisingly, before it lists the tempting possibilities of greater flexibility in working and leisure hours, the report deals with the sterner aspects: 'A result of the greater accessibility to more sources of information at higher efficiencies is the generally higher productivity of the individual.'

Already trials are under way with automatic burglar and fire alarms and automated meter reading over the phone network, and plans have been laid for an automated national banking network 'to pave the way for a cashless society'. Singapore was one of the first nations to buy the British invention of teletext to provide a computerized information service on its television channels.

On the more immediate front, a new burst of hotel building began in 1983. This, combined with the relentless replacement of old Singapore with more shop and office complexes and more blocks of flats (40,000 more state-built homes were added in 1983), meant that the construction industry contributed 20 per cent to the year's expansion. This was accelerated further in 1984 by work on the macro-engineering project, the Mass Rapid Transit (MRT) rail network, which the government hopes will thin the rush-hour use of cars – and which requires more imports of foreign labour for jobs Singaporeans are no longer keen to fill. A common sight is lorry-loads of labourers *en route* to the latest building site, and without a Chinese face among them.

Another example of the contrasts provided by the re-shaping of the city is the new Raffles complex. The historic relic, Raffles Hotel, is preserved as a tourist draw. Its long bar, cooled by ceiling fans, remains as it was in the days that Somerset Maugham depicted. But nearby the new complex rises – one 71-storey hotel, another of 28 storeys, a conference centre, and a 42-storey office block.

Tourism contributes about 8.5 per cent to the gross domestic product and 8 per cent to employment, but in 1983 the tourist business dropped by 4 per cent, the first decline in 20 years. Yet, as another sign of change, the restaurant and store trade continued to expand because of the growing incomes of Singaporeans. The tourist business established itself in the 1970s. In 1970 there were half a million visitors. By 1983 the annual total was 2.8 million – more than the island's population. The bulk came from other parts of south-east Asia, with Japan inevitably in the lead, despite a few symptoms of working-class anti-Japanese feeling, bred partly from the occupation memories of the older generation of Chinese. Britain and America head the list of Western visitors (there were 150,000 British tourists in 1983).

The island has had a Tourist Promotion Board since 1964. It is funded by a 3 per cent tax on hotels and restaurants. Nature has given Singapore few spectacular tourist attractions, apart from tropical profusion and its romantic islets. So – typically – Singapore has built its own: a bird park, with a huge walk-in aviary and man-made waterfall, classical Chinese and Japanese gardens, a botany park and an open-style zoo. Sentosa, a former British military base, has been converted into a resort island, with cable-car and monorail links. (Sentosa keeps on display the tragically useless guns that were meant to defend Singapore from a Japanese sea invasion from the south – military genius rejected the notion of a north-coast invasion.)

The Tourist Board has perhaps missed one trick through familiarity breeding contempt. In extolling the uniform equatorial temperatures of 30 degrees Centigrade maximum by day and 24 by night, it adds that 'showers are heavy but brief and refreshing'. In fact, to the uninitiated, the occasional monsoon thunder is one of Singapore's most awesome and exhilarating attractions. The sky falls, and roars as it slides, the ever clean streets become crystal-clear torrents. Raincoats are ridiculous and umbrellas frail tokens.

Back to the drier mainstream. Mr Hwang, the Economic Development Board head, summarizes the aim behind all these interlocking strategies in this way: 'We decided ten years ago that making transistor radios was not the job for us. Nor do we want workers in the rag trade. We want technical services.' It is impossible to see, he says, what will be the industries of the future – 'except that they will be computer-based.'

Mr Hwang does not merely accept that the future needs people with multi-disciplinary educations; he revels in the challenge of the change. 'The divisions are becoming blurred, the disciplines are breaking down. . . . A theologian now runs one of the best General Electric plants. So, while we are expanding traditional university work, we are also expanding extra-mural courses.'

Singapore's educational transformation is stunning. During the mid-1950s only 1 in 2 children had even primary education. Despite the fact that today nearly 90 per cent of children have to start their school careers by learning English, the English-based O-level success rate is claimed to be a quarter higher than Britain's. Dr Tay Eng Soon, minister of state for education, admits that the education system is highly competitive and meritocratic – 'but no more so than in the UK'.

The demand for graduates still exceeds the expanding supply – particularly in computer science – and the fastest-growing investment in further education is in sub-graduate technical training. There are three youth-training centres in computerized manufacturing technology, with courses ranging from design to robotics, plus technical institutes sponsored by French, German and Japanese firms. Although Britain is now only second to America in its investment in Singapore, the only formal British involvement in that training is a computer institute established in 1983 through collaboration between the British Council and the British computer company ICL.

Total enrolment in the National University rose by 13 per cent in 1983 to a total of nearly 12,000 students. The weighting of those places to meet the demand for technologists meant that the number of new science and engineering

Table 3.1 Enrolment and output of graduate, technical and skilled manpower, 1981–3

	Enrolment			Output		
	1981	1982	1983	1981	1982	1983
National University						
of Singapore	9,950	11,090	11,940	2,190	2,400	2,900
Engineering	2,140	2,120	1,890	320	350	440
Science	1,890	2,100	2,300	460	580	660
Others	5,920	6,870	7,750	1,410	1,470	1,800
Nanyang						
Technological						
Institute	–	580	1,270	–	–	–
Engineering	–	580	1,270	–	–	–
Singapore						
Polytechnic	5,460	5,580	6,180	1,440	1,720	1,820
Engineering	5,320	5,430	5,990	1,260	1,690	1,750
Others	140	150	190	180	30	70
Ngee Ann						
Polytechnic	3,140	3,790	4,840	580	750	950
Engineering	1,990	2,310	2,910	430	460	560
Computer						
studies	–	130	350	–	–	–
Others	1,150	1,350	1,580	150	290	390
Institutes of the						
Vocational and						
Industrial						
Training Board	10,090	10,690	10,320	5,820	6,650	6,780
Joint Industrial						
Training Centres/						
Institutes	1,220	1,390	1,950	580	680	520
Centres	1,220	1,240	1,570	580	680	520
Institutes	n.a.	150	380	n.a.	n.a.	n.a.

Source: Various educational institutions and Economic Development Board.

undergraduates rose by 17 per cent to a total of more than 4000. The university's 1983 output of graduates was 2900, and the two polytechnics added a further 2700 with degrees in computer studies and electronics. The multi-disciplinary emphasis was strengthened in 1983 by the introduction of degree courses combining computer science and mathematics with management studies.

At the other end of the scale, a programme called Best (Basic education for skills training) was introduced to raise the literacy and numeracy levels of unskilled and semi-skilled workers, so that they could then be retrained to operate computer-related equipment. That produced a 92 per cent success rate from the first year's 22,600 students. Companies that run retraining programmes of their own are encouraged by both grants and tax relief. Equally, firms that do no training are penalized.

One of the more democratic ways in which the Establishment tries to maintain the cohesion of Singapore society is through mass seminars at the university, in which ministers expound their departmental policies and are then questioned by the students. At one of these, in November 1982, Dr Tay summarized the government's worries about Westernization:

We are a very exposed society. The very nature of our economy, which depends on free and open contacts with many countries, means that we are open to ideas, influences, and fashions from abroad, both good and bad. We cannot invite multinational corporations to come here or encourage tourists to visit Singapore and say to them, 'Please don't bring your ideas and lifestyles to Singapore.' The fact that we have adopted English as our lingua franca . . . adds to this problem. English becomes the vehicle through which the mass media and TV purvey values from abroad, mainly the United States and the United Kingdom.

Some of the values, such as hippyism, a libertine

preoccupation with self-gratification, the cult of living for today and for myself and to hell with others, are clearly undesirable. Even people in the West are very concerned about this for their own societies. Censorship can and must be imposed to keep out such values. But it would be much better if our people have their own vigorous cultural and moral values which can withstand such attacks.

Dr Tay contrasted those who fall for the 'fads and fashions of long greasy hair' and 'soiled jeans' with an educated populace who have a taste for the arts and literature and who are 'totally unimpressed by the counter-culture emanating from the advanced countries'. He went on:

There is no real equilibrium in this silent struggle for the hearts and minds, especially of our young people. Either we strenuously make the effort in school as well as outside school, to promote good habits, good tastes, and interests or we will see an erosion of these values and their replacement by bad habits and decadent values if we simply allow the position to drift.

Our society is essentially still a conservative one. We still hold such values as thrift, hard work, keeping of one's word, honour in dealing with others, a sense of shame in not looking after our families or our parents. . . . Let us not assume that these values will always remain with us. Many great societies, even in our time, have been built on such values, the Protestant ethic, the Confucian ethic, and so on. But many of these societies are decaying. Their founding values have been overcome by libertine and hedonistic values. If it can happen to them, it can also happen to us.

It is in such examples of preaching at the populace, as much as in the economic competition to become the pivotal point of the region, that comparisons between Singapore and Hong Kong are inevitable. Mr Hwang is comparatively blunt about the uncertainties of Hong Kong's future: 'We don't like living on other people's misery, but when there are problems elsewhere, we provide a fall-back position.'

But Mr J. Y. M. Pillay, chairman of Singapore Airlines and permanent secretary of the Finance Ministry (not so bizarre a combination of jobs in Singapore's small cadre of top people), was more subtle when he addressed a Hong Kong conference on the economic prospects for the 1990s.

Mr Pillay argued that the similarities were more significant than the differences. 'Our fortunes are closely related. Trouble in one place cannot benefit the other in the long run. Indeed, this is true for the entire Asia–Pacific region.' He added:

> Hong Kong is somewhat more gung-ho than Singapore, which to Hong Kong eyes may appear hidebound by rules, regulations, and laws. Singapore, nonetheless, has a long way to go before reaching the absurd regulatory levels of western countries. Our rules, or that portion of them that intrigues visitors, circumscribe personal rather than corporate behaviour. . . .
>
> In manufacturing, the nimble-footed Hong Kong entrepreneur has struck out on his own. Singapore prefers to work through large institutions: the government itself, multinational corporations, joint ventures with foreign establishments, and some home-grown giants. We are therefore more slow-moving in responding to changes in fortunes outside our control, but perhaps steadier on the tiller.

In that subtle defence, Mr Pillay skated around one central strand of doubt about Singapore's long-term success: the comparative lack of home-grown innovation. Given solid world recovery from the recession – and given sufficient progress by its poorer neighbours to dampen the fires of jealousy – then Singapore looks set to consolidate its pivotal position as the 'brain industry' centre of its immediate region.

But can it range beyond that in the 1990s, particularly in gaining a major share of high-tech trade to China? Within a quarter-century it has advanced from slum-ridden, education-starved colonialism to rich industrialism. Now it is moving fast into the post-industrial industries. But that second advance, like the first, still relies on inward investment by American, Japanese and European multinationals.

The signs of Singaporean invention or entrepreneurial innovation in fields such as computer science are small so far. Officials of the Economic Development Board deny being worried about this. 'We've never made the distinction between incoming and local in value-added industry, as long as the value-added is in Singapore,' said one.

Nevertheless, Mr Lee and his co-leaders show a clearer understanding than one usually finds in Europe or America that the acceleration in technological change in the late twentieth century is also accelerating the historical drift of economic power from one region of the world to another. Mr Pillay summed it up:

> The same rapid [Asian] growth rate of the 60s and 70s cannot be sustained in the next two decades, even allowing for explosive growth in the information-processing industry. . . . Sooner or later another region of the world, yet to be identified, will overtake us. Will we then settle down to middle-aged prosperity and all the dangers that situation holds? That is the challenge for the 90s and beyond.

Note on sources

As with all the other chapters of this book, the vital information comes from talking to people. But for the choice aphorism about Einstein and some of the earlier economic history I am indebted to Professor Tom Stonier's *The Wealth of Information* (Methuen, London, 1983). The bread-and-butter statistics come from the annual reports and surveys of the Singapore Economic Development Board, the Singapore Ministry of Trade and Industry and the Ministry of Culture, the Singapore Telecommunications Authority, and the Lloyds Bank annual 'Economic Report' on Singapore.

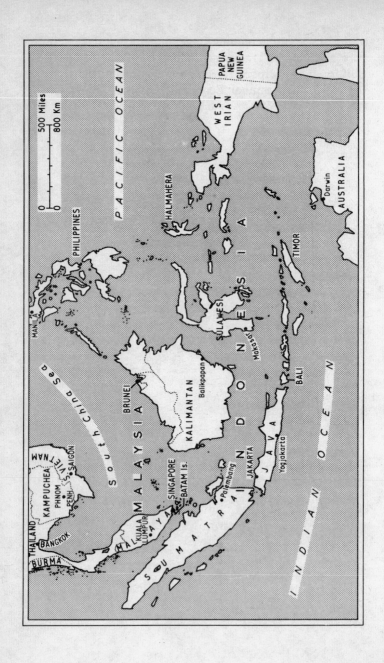

4 INDONESIA

ROD CHAPMAN

Foreign tourists may be seen at performances of the *wayang*, the Javanese shadow theatre, agonizing over whether they should watch from behind or in front of the screen. In the event, it makes little difference: few are going to be able to follow the plot, identify the characters or appreciate the skill of the puppeteer.

The analogy of the *wayang* is much used but always apt in dealing with the Indonesian socio-economic system. Indonesia's diversity and the mysterious and mystical way of doing things militate against predictions on future development. For every argument supporting the theory that Indonesia will achieve the industrial miracles of neighbouring Singapore or of Japan, an equally cogent case can be made that the divergent and violent forces within the society will sabotage President Suharto's hard-won unity at some point. Riots in Jakarta in the autumn of 1984 and the subsequent reversion to calm served warning of the latent dichotomy.

Western leaders and financiers heaped plaudits on Indonesia at the London economic summit in June 1984 for its imposition of voluntary austerity measures in the previous two years to overcome the crisis caused by a fall in world oil prices. But the blow to development aspirations may yet prove too severe for the country's burgeoning population of nearly 160 million which makes the far-flung archipelago the fifth most populous nation in the world.

President Suharto, the 'Father of Development', realizes that his pot-pourri of a country is at a crossroads in its industrial evolution and has called on Indonesians to 'nurture the fighting spirit in order to overcome development difficulties'. Unlike the other countries in this survey, Indonesia is still predominantly underdeveloped, with a frail industrial base on which to support the hopes of the island population. The economy is one of tenuous rural subsistence for most Indonesians.

As with many other Third World countries, Indonesia suffers from glaring social differences. The most worrying chasms are not those separating Indonesia from the rich men's club of industrialized nations, but those dividing different groups within Indonesian society.

Javanese legend has it that the navel of the universe is to be found on one of the island's many mountains. Allowing for legendary exaggeration, Indonesia is certainly the Pacific basin country with the most natural potential to become a regional and even a world industrial power.

The archipelago stretches over a shimmering pattern of nearly 13,700 islands and water (Indonesians count water as part of their territory) as broad as the USA. The volcanoes, rain forests and broad plains which make up the landscape provide an abundance of oil, gas, coal, minerals, timber, rubber, rice and a host of other saleable commodities. Man has been living in these environs almost for ever, as proved by the discovery of fossils of ape men and of a precursor of *Homo erectus* in central Java. In more modern times, Indonesia has absorbed Chinese, Indian, Arabian and European ethnic groups, their cultures and religions.

The resources, the land and the young, inexpensive labour force – some two-thirds of the population is under 25 – are much coveted by countries like Japan and Singapore, whose expansion is in danger of imploding because of lack of space. As will be seen later, joint ventures are proliferating between the four countries discussed in this book.

If variety were the panacea for economic and industrial progress, Indonesia would be better placed than any other developing country in the world. But President Suharto, a canny Javanese villager himself, appreciates that such diversity will always prove hard to manage.

By almost the same token, the oil riches of the 1970s have brought with them a form of the Midas touch. Jakarta, the prism through which many Westerners see Indonesia, has the murky appearance of the ugliest of Western industrial towns. Pollution rasps the eyes and ears on the congested roads, which are so clogged by cars that Jakarta is to ban the *becaks*, the leisurely trishaws. The traffic jam is the microcosm of post-oil-boom urban society in Indonesia, with urchins from the proliferating shanty towns wading in among the cars to sell newspapers and cigarettes to the new rich.

President Suharto's managerial matrix embodies an Indonesian version of *e pluribus unum*. The state crest is a fearsome eagle beneath which is the motto 'Bhinneka Tunggal Ika', or 'We are many but we are one'. On the eagle's chest is a shield representing the five principles of the Pancasila, the state philosophy of Indonesia.

The principles are not dissimilar to those of other national bills of rights. They are: a belief in God (the majority of Indonesians are Muslim, but Bali is a Hindu island and Buddhism and Christianity also flourish); nationalism; a village-based democracy; humanitarianism; and a social justice which provides food for all.

In practice President Suharto's so-called New Order government has used the incantation of Pancasila to cover a concentration of power. The hierarchies of the army, the Muslim religion and the Javanese heartland have ruthlessly welded together a base with the encouragement of the president, who uses the myth and magic of the *wayang* and other Javanese traditions to reinforce his position as the absolute ruler. Their use of power has shown scant respect for several credos of the Pancasila, though possible signs of change are now emerging.

President Suharto came to power following the cathartic period of blood-letting in 1966. The previous year, Sukarno's 'year of living dangerously', marked the sad end of the first post-colonial phase. It also saw the demise of the man who had declared Indonesia independent in 1945 and fought off the bitter attempts of the Dutch to regain control of their former colony until they at last recognized independence at the end of 1948.

(The three years of Japanese occupation at the end of World War II struck a sour note of Asian disunity. The occupiers proved every bit as repressive with the Indonesians – despite their promotion of the nascent nationalism – and with Sukarno and the national language Bahasa Indonesia, as they were with British and other prisoners of war. Indonesian raw materials were exploited for the refurbishment of the Tokyo war machine.)

The Indonesia Sukarno took over from Dutch rule had little to commend it as a prototype for Third World development. The Dutch, whatever the vague, lingering affection for them in the islands today, had been at their patronizing, colonial worst in Indonesia, treating the islanders as less than children. There had been minimal education for the Indonesians and no training for administrative or industrial jobs. Additionally, the fighting of the period immediately before the transfer of sovereignty had seen the destruction of many of the textile mills – and had witnessed an angry clash between Sukarno and the PKI (the Indonesian Communist Party) which was to sow the seeds for the events of 1965–6.

In the next twenty years Sukarno built a reputation as a Third World leader to rank alongside the likes of Nkrumah, Nyerere and Castro. His wayward charisma helped the process towards political and economic unity which Suharto has consolidated, but at a considerable price. Internal violence which has always been endemic within the archipelago welled up into the Sumatran uprising of 1958, and Sukarno aimed a campaign of external hatred at Malaysia.

Sukarno's power-mongering took various forms including the abolition of political parties in favour of 'guided democracy', in which the Bung, the president, himself was the guide, picking the National Council himself. His public diatribes became increasingly anti-Western, although – in true Indonesian spirit – his regime bore little comparison with that of other supposedly left-wing Third World governments.

The economy by the early 1960s had reached a state of disarray of Argentinian proportions, with three-digit inflation rates and much squandering of official funds. Indonesian cities, particularly Jakarta, still bear the architectural imprint. Monolithic, Soviet-style hotels and stadiums abound, along with curious statues on traffic islands at roundabouts. The motorized mayhem of central Jakarta takes place in the lee of the Freedom monument, more commonly known as 'Sukarno's last erection'.

Suharto, an increasingly respected figure in the military during the struggle for independence and then through the Sukarno years, came to the fore when the abortive Communist coup against the ageing Sukarno was put down with unparalleled savagery by the army and army-backed groups of Muslim youths. The PKI and the army had been sparring for some time, but there had been little suggestion of the annihilation of the Communists that took place in 1965–6. Estimates at the time put the death toll of Communists at one million; this has since been revised down to 500,000. But certainly Indonesia's rivers ran with blood.

President Suharto therefore inherited the same sort of mess as his predecessor – but one perpetrated by Indonesians. His task was to restitch the fabric of political and economic unity, with the emphasis on the latter, since the Indonesian economy was once again in shreds.

On the political side the changes have been barely apparent. The army has been running the show at the presidential behest, with the head of the armed forces, General Benny Murdhani, becoming the power behind the throne.

In spring 1984 his troops began a new campaign against the Fretilin guerrillas in East Timor, the former Portuguese island on the outer rim of the archipelago which Indonesia invaded in 1975. There have also been clashes with troops from Papua New Guinea along the border with Irian Jaya, the most easterly of Indonesia's many islands.

On the home political front President Suharto is accused of running a one-party state, and that party is Golkar, the government's political arm which was created by the army under Sukarno. The Golkar congress last October launched what could be a far-reaching initiative by Indonesian standards: new civilian leaders were elected in a possible move towards civilian rule after Suharto retires, if the military gives the nod. Yet u   · Suharto, political opposition has been stifled: the appointment of retired general Sudharmono as Golkar chairman at its last party congress gave Suharto a strong henchman.

But, just as the army appears ready to open up the system slightly, its troops are accused of being the 'mysterious killers' or death-squads responsible for murdering an estimated 10,000 people over the two years to 1984. The victims are urban criminals, whose proliferation has been caused by the deterioration of social conditions in the city slums.

It is these conditions which future development strategy will seek to improve. 'I think, if one looks at Indonesia's progress over the last 15 years it has been miraculous in so many ways,' says one leading Western oil man of long standing; 'political and economic stability has been achieved and the confidence of foreign investors has been built up: from our vantage point, it's a good investment market – a lot of credit goes to the leadership.'

While President Suharto has exercised political control through the army and Golkar, his economic instrument has been the Repelita, or five-year plan. Foreign businessmen say that Indonesia is the antithesis of Hong Kong, in that the government's hand is visible in every conceivable deal.

Table 4.1 Government development expenditure, by sector[1] (billions of *rupiah*[2])

Sector	First Plan Cumulative actual 1969/70– 1973/74		Second Plan Cumulative actual 1974/75– 1978/79	
	Total	%	Total	%
Agriculture and irrigation	267.8	21.7	1,745.2	19.1
Industry, mining and energy	193.7	15.8	1,653.4	18.1
Transportation and communications	261.4	21.2	1,631.8	17.9
Regional and local development[3]	210.1	17.0	1,024.5	11.2
Public enterprises[4]	71.3	5.8	790.0	8.7
Education	83.8	6.8	758.2	8.3
Health and family planning	27.3	2.2	262.0	2.9
Others	117.5	9.5	1,261.4	13.8
Total	1,232.8	100.0	9,126.5	100.0

Sector	Third Plan					
	Actual 1982/83		Budget 1983/84		Cumulative planned 1979/80– 1983/84	
	Total[5]	%	Total	%	Total	%
Agriculture and irrigation	2,931	12.6	1,324	14.2	3,048.9	14.0
Industry, mining and energy	1,671	22.7	1,564	16.8	4,117.9	18.8
Transportation and communications	876	11.9	1,307	14.1	3,384.3	15.5
Regional and local development[3]	711	9.7	783	8.4	2,142.9	9.8
Public enterprises[4]	281	3.8	265	2.9	370.3	1.7
Education	704	9.6	1,329	14.3	2,276.8	10.4
Health and family planning	259	3.5	344	3.7	829.1	3.8
Others	1,927	26.2	2,374	25.6	5,679.2	26.0
Total	7,360	100.0	9,290	100.0	21,849.4	100.0

Sources: Third Five-Year Development Plan, Bappenas and Ministry of Finance.

Notes:
[1] Includes only development expenditure of the central government.
[2] From 1971 to 1978 US $1.00 = Rp 415; from November 1978 until August 1983 the value of the *rupiah* fluctuated between Rp 625 and Rp 988.6 per US $1.00.
[3] The portion of development expenditure by provincial and local governments financed by the central government.
[4] The portion of development expenditure by government-owned enterprises financed by the central government.
[5] Figures reflect rounding.

Since the late 1960s, the New Order government has used the Repelita as the main form of state interventionism in the fledgling economy. The first and second, lasting from 1969 to 1979, concentrated on developing the crucial agricultural sector, improving living standards and starting to build an industrial infrastructure.

Their efficacy was mitigated by the collapse of the state oil company Pertamina in 1975 with foreign debts of $10 billion. A government bail-out followed, of course, but the affair dealt a body blow to the Indonesian economy which was tantamount to a rescheduling. The Pertamina crisis followed the rise and fall of one of Indonesia's new-style entrepreneurs, Ibnu Sutowo, whose dealings were enmeshed in corruption, delusions of industrial grandeur and chronic overspending which pushed up the national inflation rate in the mid-1970s. Worse still for Indonesia's national pride, Sutowo had the ear of the 'Father of Development', who only withdrew his backing at the last.

The third Repelita again backed agriculture and labour-intensive industries such as textiles, though the manufacturing sector was nurtured increasingly behind closed doors. Nevertheless the whole edifice was still built on booming oil revenues which reached their zenith at the end of the OPEC decade of the 1970s, a strength which turned into a vulnerability when oil prices began to stagnate in 1982.

Oil revenues helped Indonesia chalk up real growth rates of 9.9 per cent in 1980 and 7.6 per cent in 1981. At the end of that year, the current account showed a $2.1 billion surplus, with oil contributing some 70 per cent of government revenues. The following year OPEC's decision to impose production quotas for member countries in the face of a global oil glut wiped $2.5 billion from net Indonesian oil-export earnings. When the oil group cut $5 a barrel from its marker price in March 1983, President Suharto completed a package of austerity measures which were to earn him kudos in the international banking community and elsewhere in the West.

The 1983–4 budget had already begun to bite the bullet, and domestic subsidies were cut on fertilizers, pesticides, food and fuel products. The last is of vital importance to rural Indonesia and to the poorer sections of the urban community. While the rural electrification programme is slowly spreading electricity to the villages, kerosene fuels the lamps which are the countless eyes of rural Indonesia's night.

At the end of March 1983 President Suharto, backing the line of the American-educated ministers and officials in the economics ministries and in Bappenas, the National Development Agency, devalued the *rupiah* by 27.6 per cent against the US dollar. 'Indonesians are almost Gladstonian in their housekeeping approach,' muses one British observer; 'they were determined to keep their debt service burden comfortable.' Nevertheless Indonesia, as foreign bankers are wont to point out, is no Mexico or Brazil: foreign debts had reached some $20 billion but repayments were spread out over several years.

The next step, in May 1983, was the rescheduling of forty-seven capital projects worth about $21 billion. Three of the four largest were in the energy sector: the Musi refinery, the Plaji aromatics centre and Exxon's olefins complex. The rescheduling package created much confusion, having been hatched by a small group of economics ministers with no consultation or warning and amid the customary Indonesian secrecy. But it came as little surprise, arriving hard on the heels of an influential World Bank report suggesting that foreign-exchange-intensive projects be re-examined.

'They were a series of tough remedial measures, but Indonesia needed to change gear,' says one Western observer in Jakarta; 'the country had a very ambitious development programme which was brewed in the late 1970s when there was an enormous increase in oil revenues.'

The austerity measures did not stop there. In June 1983

the government launched a banking liberalization package, allowing the banks to set their own interest rates for the first time, exempting foreign currency time deposits from tax and removing ceilings on bank loans. The government also drew up plans to introduce a value added tax as the preliminary phase to launching a complete overhaul of Indonesia's outdated and complex taxation system – which is seen as discouraging foreign investment.

The taxation system is also considered to encourage the corruption which the vast Indonesian bureaucracy wears as its shroud. Behind it, lowly paid officials, whose salaries were frozen as part of the president's draconian programme to retrieve some of his development ambitions, look for sweeteners. These are slipped into the machine to obtain the myriad forms and stamps needed by businesses; clearance of air freight, for example, following the imposition of exorbitant import duties, often takes seven to nine days from its arrival.

One of the few legacies of Dutch colonialism is that to work for the government guarantees good social standing. However, clerks in the Jakarta ministries are paid considerably less than their counterparts in the private sector and attempt to make up the difference accordingly. Meanwhile in rural districts, the shake-down by minor *mafiosi* is becoming prevalent again. A bus I travelled on in 1983 through the rubber estates of Sumatra was boarded by a young thug with a sizeable spider in his hair who proceeded to take contributions from all the passengers and the driver.

Such petty criminals, with their tattooes denoting membership of a criminal sect, risk becoming victims of the 'mysterious killers'. A less covert campaign has been launched by the government to root out bureaucratic corruption. It has netted only a few small fish so far; cynics say that that is as much as it will ever do. However, a campaign has also begun to eliminate the red tape which ties the clerks to corruption, though it is widely alleged that the corruption reaches right up to the president's own family.

The aim of the comprehensive measures was to right the floundering ship of state and to reduce Indonesian dependency on oil exports. It was a vital prelude to the fourth Repelita, launched in April 1984, which could be the most important so far – the adjustment sideways before the next leap forward.

The measures have certainly had the desired effect in many areas. Real growth is estimated at over 4 per cent for 1983, following a drop to 2.2 per cent in 1982. A current account deficit which was up to $7 billion in 1982–3 and threatening to leap to $11 billion in the following financial year dropped back to $4–4.5 billion.

With the immediate threat to progress mitigated, the president and his ministers have emphasized industrial growth in the new five-year plan. Yet the pervasive agricultural sector and the oil and gas industry will still need to be supported. The former employs well over half the labour force, the latter accounts for over 60 per cent of state earnings (despite the emphasis on Jakarta's most popular acronym these days: NOE, standing for non-oil exports).

The problem, as always, for the president is how the government can push through a new development programme which will mean sufficient things to all of the archipelago's sub-groups. As one international official says, the harsh side of the austerity programme is that 'Indonesians in general are suffering: people are suffering less in the rural areas because of the good rice crop, but the urban poor were probably worst hit by the price increases on domestic fuel and other commodities.' Whatever the impression given by the hotel and restaurant zone of Jakarta, Indonesia's per capita gross domestic product (GDP) is less than $600 per annum, low in the Asian stakes.

President Suharto himself has been attempting to rally the national spirit again, while warning that progress will be hard under the fourth Repelita. He has said that the plan, though limited by the effects of the world recession, would be decisive in determining future development plans. But the structural foundations would be reinforced during the fifth Repelita – so that, during the sixth, development would be able to take off and 'attain self-propelling growth'.

If the fourth Repelita provides the framework for the next five years, different groupings within the government will be jostling to set their stamp on the ideology – a process already encouraged by Suharto in the latter half of the third Repelita. The Berkeley *mafia* of American-educated economists won out over the austerity measures. They are headed by Professor Ali Wardhana, the co-ordinating minister for the economy, finance, industry and development supervision. His mentor was Dr Widjojo Nisistrato, the former minister, and his leading supporter within the government is the minister for national development planning and Bappenas, Professor J. B. Sumarlin.

But there are other powerful groups. The finance minister Dr Radius Prawiro and the Bank of Indonesia are advised by a triumvirate of international banks, Lazard Freres, Warburgs and Kuhn Loeb Lehman, who bring out influential reports on Indonesia, and by the Harvard group of economists. The industry ministry looks to a growing group of Indonesian engineers.

And there is the research and technology minister Dr Bachruddin Habibie, who currently has the ear of the president and was brought back by him from West Germany to help build the president's dreams. Dr Habibie is in a group of one, but he has already ensured that Indonesia has the only native aircraft industry in the region. President Suharto dismissed cautious comments on his country's future at a recent function with a wave of the hand and the comment, 'Yes, but we can build aeroplanes.'

Battle has been joined most vigorously between Dr Habibie and the economists. The latter argue that Indonesia should look to labour-intensive industries as a means of keeping its young workforce content. Dr Habibie maintains that the country needs to push ahead with technological development in order not to be left further and further behind the industrialized world.

Dr Habibie's controversial development theory has its focal point at Bandung in central Java, an apt spot. It is the home of the renowned Institute of Technology and the base for radical intellectuals such as those behind Suharto's *Putsch* which replaced the 'old order' government of President Sukarno in 1966. The only irony is that the mountain overlooking Bandung is known locally as the upturned boat: it looks down on a gleaming new aircraft factory.

The Nurtanio plant was set up in 1976, when it employed some 500 people. In 1984 it employs almost 10,000 and produces a range of helicopters and medium-sized passenger planes. The next phase will be to develop relatively large planes and new technologies.

The jewel in Nurtanio's crown is the CN-235 turbo-prop passenger plane, a 34- to 38-seater which had its roll-out amid a fanfare of publicity in autumn 1983. It was co-designed and built by CASA of Spain, but the Indonesian factory intends to increase local manufacture of components until it reaches 100 per cent. Most of the employees are under 25 and locally engaged, which means intensive on-the-job training in aircraft manufacture.

Nurtanio already has a number of licensing and joint-venture agreements and is looking for more. It makes the Messerschmitt-Boelkow-Blohm NBO-105 helicopter, and the AS-332 Super Puma and AS-330 helicopter under licence from Aerospatiale of France. Production on a new Bell helicopter will begin this year, and Nurtanio has a co-operation agreement with Boeing under which it hopes to become the American company's south-east Asian contractor by 1986-7. It would also like to get into the military aviation market. A British Aerospace team visited Bandung in 1983 for talks on the Hawk trainer aircraft.

Just as Bandung is one of the few venues visited by Western prospectors in search of the new industrial grail of the Pacific basin – a team of US Congressmen recently declared it was the most impressive facility they had seen in the region – Dr Habibie trots the globe looking for new backers. He has signed a memorandum to establish an Indonesia–Japan Forum for Science and Technology to sponsor joint projects, and renewed a similar agreement with the United States.

One of the more persuasive arguments for the technology-led strategy is the peculiarity of Indonesia's geographical and social needs. Air and sea transport are vital for the faltering *transmigrasi* (transmigration) programme, under which some 2 million people were moved from 1979 to 1984 from the densely populated islands of Java and Bali to the outer islands like Irian Jaya. Dr Habibie's planes could be the new *becaks* of the islands. Nurtanio has a captive market, and most of the 120 initial orders for the CN-235 at the roll-out had come from local airlines.

Other schemes in Dr Habibie's growing empire include the PT Pal state shipyard near Surabaya, whose plans to buy $500 million of Boeing hydrofoils were scotched by the government's rescheduling plans; PT Pindad, the army defence industry centre and Puspitek, the Centre for Development of Research, Science and Technology.

But perhaps the most fascinating project is the development of Batam Island, just south of Singapore, as a regional industrial centre particularly suitable for technological start-ups. Indonesia and Singapore agreed in 1980 to develop the island jointly, and President Suharto and the Singaporean prime minister Lee Kuan Yew had further discussions on this joint effort at the end of last year. Dr Habibie said then that the ultimate purpose was to ease congestion in Singapore's port facilities, to serve as a storage and trans-shipment point for goods marketed in the Middle East and the Asia/Pacific region – and to become a centre for high-technology and other industries.

If successful, the port/city concept could be used throughout Indonesia. One of the possibilities under study is that Indonesia should develop a new 'gateway policy', using coastal ports for different development functions and decentralizing further. The Planning Research Corporation has been looking into the potential for development and free trade zones like Batam at Dr Habibie's behest.

Dr Habibie's opponents within the government question the wisdom of the technology drive at a time when the country is undergoing a period of belt-tightening. Funding for Nurtanio, whose ventures have cost nearly $200 million to develop so far, comes from a special budget which was not cut when the forty-seven development projects were rescheduled. One international development official in Jakarta comments that 'Nurtanio and PT Pal are the exceptions rather than the rule: these technological enterprises could be exactly the thing Indonesia is worst at.'

While the president is still backing new technological efforts, the fourth Repelita should focus on strengthening the base of industrialization. Industrial growth stagnated in the early 1980s, and the industrial sector accounts for a miserable 15.8 per cent of GDP, the lowest figure among the ASEAN countries.

The new five-year plan sets a target of 19.4 per cent for industry's contribution to the national GDP by 1989. Projections for job creation have been revised upwards from earlier estimates, and call for 1.4 million jobs to be created in industry over the duration of the Repelita, 930,000 of them in small-scale manufacturing. President Suharto has gone on record as saying that as long as Indonesia remains incapable of making machinery and has to rely on foreign expertise and equipment, it will not have a strong industrial base.

But past policies have discouraged many potential foreign investors, and it may be a difficult trick to put them into reverse. Each year under the third Repelita the BKPM (the Investment Co-ordinating Board) reduced the industrial sectors open to foreign investment as domestic producers emerged. Even with high-technology joint-ventures, Indonesians have to hold 51 per cent of the shares ten years

Table 4.2 Percentage distribution of gross domestic product at constant 1973 market prices, by industrial origin

Industrial origin	1979	1980	1981[1]	1982[2]
Agriculture, livestock, forestry and fisheries				
Farm food crops	18.78	18.56	18.76	18.62
Farm non-food crops	3.96	3.73	3.56	3.72
Estate crops	2.27	2.08	2.02	2.31
Livestock and products	1.98	1.90	1.82	1.87
Forestry	3.32	2.76	2.04	1.59
Fishery	1.72	1.63	1.61	1.66
Mining and quarrying	10.30	9.26	8.87	7.62
Manufacturing industries	13.73	15.26	15.58	15.42
Construction	5.54	5.72	5.97	6.15
Wholesale and retail trade	16.54	16.58	16.94	17.52
Transport and communications	5.51	5.46	5.62	5.81
Banking and other financial intermediaries	1.76	1.86	1.92	2.10
Public administration and defence	7.92	8.70	8.92	9.04
Services	2.99	2.79	2.64	2.65
Others	3.68	3.71	3.73	3.92
Gross domestic product	100.00	100.00	100.00	100.00

Source: Central Bureau of Statistics.

Notes:
[1] Revised figures.
[2] Preliminary figures.

after start-up. Foreign firms are forbidden by decree from owning estates, and recent lobbying has failed to change the president's mind on the controversial issue of land ownership.

The government brought in a policy of counter-purchase in 1982 as a ploy to increase the non-oil exports. It stipulates that foreign companies awarded government contracts buy Indonesian goods to the equivalent value. It was resisted initially – and the Japanese, the dominant foreign investors, did not cave in until the end of the year – but became a *fait accompli* as intermediaries like Citibank began to put together deals for suppliers and potential buyers.

Table 4.3 Percentage distribution of gross domestic product at current and constant 1973 market prices, by expenditure

Type of expenditure	1979	1980	1981[1]	1982[2]
(at current market prices)				
Private consumption expenditure	60.93	60.52	65.82	69.88
General Government consumption expenditure	11.66	10.32	10.71	11.46
Gross domestic fixed capital formation	20.93	20.87	21.39	22.58
Export of goods and services	30.07	30.47	27.63	22.38
Less: import of goods and services	23.59	22.18	25.55	26.30
Gross domestic product	100.00	100.00	100.00	100.00
(at constant 1973 market prices)				
Private consumption expenditure	77.38	79.39	85.86	86.79
General Government consumption expenditure	13.23	13.34	13.61	14.41
Gross domestic fixed capital formation	23.97	25.93	26.70	29.51
Export of goods and services	17.92	15.39	13.92	11.72
Less: import of goods and services	32.50	34.05	40.09	42.43
Gross domestic product	100.00	100.00	100.00	100.00

Source: Central Bureau of Statistics.

Notes:
[1] Revised figures.
[2] Preliminary figures.

Indonesia's first counter-purchase deal following the announcement of the policy was unveiled in August 1982 as the result of several months of negotiations, and is one of the largest deals ever concluded internationally. It involved an agreement between the Department of Trade and twelve foreign companies for the supply of $154 million of fertilizer. The first full year of active counter-purchasing produced purchases of some $600 million, according to most estimates. 'But I suspect that it would be hard to substantiate incremental exports,' says one Western businessman involved.

Indonesia has become the leading participant in north–south counter-trade. But the spread of this and of import-substitution measures has often tended to foster the inefficiency and leaky quality control of new Indonesian manufacturing industries, which have also been protected by high tariff barriers. The presence of a large and willing domestic market for indigenous products cuts both ways. 'If a manufacturer here is making jogging shoes of inferior quality and selling them all, it is hard to convince him of the need for higher standards,' says one Western businessman.

These and other factors have undoubtedly deterred many would-be investors. And the president has been on the stump in recent months declaring that Indonesia must strive for self-sufficiency in areas like the production of chemicals and fertilizers. Yet Professor Sumarlin stressed on presenting the new Repelita that the role of both domestic and foreign investors will assume greater importance under the new plan.

The effect of these factors and of the government's decision to postpone its proposed tax reforms was seen by most observers as one of the main reasons for an alarming drop in new domestic and foreign investments in the early part of 1984. Embarrassingly for the government, disclosure of this stagnation occurred at the very time that posses of Indonesians were visiting foreign countries trying to interest them in the new Repelita.

Figures released in July 1984 showed that no new foreign investment project was licensed in the first quarter of 1984, compared with twelve projects which had been approved at the same stage in 1983. The number of domestic investments also slumped dramatically, from 47 to just 7.

Overall only $2.5 billion had been invested in Indonesia by the end of June 1984, against a target of $6.5 billion. Mr Suhartoyo, chairman of the Capital Investment Co-ordinating Board which published the figures, claimed the down-turn was because a rush of investors had taken advantage of the government's 'tax holiday' in the previous year, and that investors were now awaiting the new tax reforms.

Even when the investment does get through, it is not always used efficiently, according to no less a source than the 'Father of Development'. In June 1984, President Suharto called for improved efficiency in the implementation of national development projects financed by industrialized countries and international groups participating in IGGI (the Inter-Governmental Group on Indonesia). IGGI has agreed to provide more than $2.4 billion of aid for 1984–5.

In all, Indonesia is looking for a total investment of $16.2 billion to be ploughed into the economy from 1984 to 1989 if the Repelita is to achieve its targets of an annual growth in GDP of 5 per cent and a 9.5 per cent increase in industrial output.

These figures are thought too cautious by some Western agencies, including the World Bank – which is understood to reckon that the economy should grow by 6 to 7 per cent a year to enable Indonesia to cope with its employment problems. As one foreign observer points out,

Indonesia really has no choice but to go for growth: the short-term crisis is now over, and this was almost 100 per cent attributable to international events beyond their control, but the real issue for the Indonesians is long-term growth – they have to think about how they can get back to the growth patterns (of the early 1980s) and absorb the enormous ambitions of the labour force.

The acid test for the new Repelita, which is held officially to be a set of guidelines but is of almost mystical importance to the president, is whether it can absorb the almost 10 million workers who are expected to enter the labour force over the next five years. Of all the figures bandied around by officialdom, those for unemployment are the most chimerical.

Officially unemployment was estimated in 1983 at 4.2 per cent. But this means workers with less than four fours work a week. Underemployment is put at 35 per cent. On the other hand Indonesian resourcefulness creates jobs out of nothing. In the cities men collect cigarette stubs to recycle as new cigarettes or use in the process of batik-making. Tourism has engendered a new breed of charming, English-speaking hustlers in locations like Bali, the Paradise Island, or the central Javanese city of Yogyakarta – where language has been refined to the single statement/question/exclamation 'batik'.

Several of Indonesia's growth and employment dilemmas still come together in the energy sector – the nation's breadwinner, no matter what pump priming is going into NOE. Indonesia, like many other oil producers, has seen most of its major oil discoveries developed and is likely to see a decline in production over the next two decades. But judicious incentives slipped the way of the oil companies could put off the fateful day when the oil runs out.

However, despite the impressive figures – Indonesia is one of the world's top ten oil exporters and the leading producer of LNG (liquefied natural gas) – the demographic explosion is theatening to put paid to self-sufficiency. The energy minister Subroto told a conference in Jakarta in 1984 that Indonesia could become an oil importer if it did not succeed in reducing its domestic fuel consumption. This would pose a 'medium-term threat' to the country's development.

In a bizarre acknowledgement of the uneven pattern of development during the oil boom, Indonesia is now to discourage the use of private cars through a series of measures including a progressive taxation system on the possession of two or more cars. Rusmin Nuryadin, the communications minister, revealed that some areas in urban centres will be declared toll areas for private cars during the new development plan, which will also seek to promote public transport.

Domestic industries will be encouraged to use gas and coal under the fourth Repelita, with the gas industry being linked with the engineering and factory-equipment industry to meet the energy needs of capital goods production which the government hopes will expand. Under an energy diversification programme over half the national energy budget of $12 billion will be used to try to double electricity capacity by 1989, while the state coal company Tambang Batubara will attempt to double coal output to 500,000 tonnes this year. Indonesia intends to build its first nuclear plant in central Java by 1989 – while the irrepressible Dr Habibie has been discussing plans with visiting Finns to develop an experimental peat-fired power plant in Sumatra.

Whatever the fears about growing domestic oil consumption, Indonesia is still the only major oil exporter of the region, though new finds in Australia and China could change the long-term exporting picture. It is the only Asian member of OPEC, and Dr Subroto has exerted considerable influence at the crisis meetings of that organization over the past couple of years, which have attempted to adopt a strategy to cope with the world oil glut.

But there were doubts and rumours about Indonesia's OPEC membership in 1984. Under OPEC's system of voluntary production restraints designed to firm up the oil markets, Indonesia accepted a quota of 1.3 million barrels a day over 1983–4 – which has been the main factor in declining oil revenues. Oil exports brought in $14 billion during the 1983–4 fiscal year, about $2 billion below the target set by the last Repelita (although exports leapt by 32 per cent in the first quarter of 1984).

The squeeze on revenues has tested Indonesia's loyalty to OPEC, and oil-industry sources say output has frequently strayed above the quota level, though only going as high as 1.4/1.6 million barrels a day. Early in 1984 Dr Subroto affirmed that Indonesia was averaging a production figure in line with the OPEC quota, after some reports had apparently misquoted him as giving total production as 1.6 million barrels a day.

President Suharto even went through a ritualistic declaration that Indonesia will remain a member of OPEC, when reports were swirling around the oil markets to the effect that several member countries, including Iran, Algeria and Nigeria, were planning to leave the organization. It does not seem likely that Indonesia would wish to leave at present, but Dr Subroto has predicted in the past that OPEC could decentralize into regional producing groups – whose Asian affiliate, of course, would be headed by Indonesia. Oil exploration efforts elsewhere in the region and greater industrial co-operation between its countries could bring this idea nearer to fruition in the 1990s. Japan, Singapore and South Korea are already some of Indonesia's main customers for oil and gas.

As Dr Subroto has admitted in a candid moment, any loss of oil-exporting capacity would prevent the country's national development from reaching take-off stage during the sixth Repelita starting in 1994. Total production peaked in 1977 at 1.69 million barrels a day, but capacity is still around that level or slightly higher: oilmen in Jakarta claim it could rise to 1.8 million barrels a day, not the 2 million barrels occasionally mentioned by the government.

Nevertheless to preserve that capacity the Indonesian government has to maintain good relations with the major oil companies, all of which are constantly looking for new incentives from developing countries with oil reserves, in a multinational oil game in which one country is played off against another.

Most of these companies currently view Indonesia as a good bet. The head of one oil giant says,

> The investment climate is one of the best in the world, and the technical potential is strong . . . given that people are willing to come here and explore, the Indonesian government is helpful: I am hopeful that we will retain the incentives we have had since 1977, when they produced an acceptable set of fiscal terms – which produced an upsurge in exploration activity.

In all, 75 foreign oil contractors are now operating in Indonesia, with 20 already producing oil from their allocated fields. Oil exploration in the islands dates back to the latter half of the last century, but discoveries have proliferated in the past couple of decades: 290 new oil fields were found from 1970 to 1982. The big producing areas are Sumatra, central Java and East Kalimantan but the companies are now pushing out to 'drill in the middle of nowhere', in the words of one Jakarta oil executive.

Most recent finds have been smaller than those of the 1970s, and will need more exploration and development work to bring their oil on stream. 'It's a long, slow progress to set up here,' says one old oil hand in Jakarta; 'a lot of oil companies would be reluctant to come here because of the problems, but you have to be here to win anything.' Drilling crews may be required to sit out in the jungles of Sumatra for months, or grapple with the mountains and other difficulties of terrain out in Irian Jaya, where there is now a fair amount of prospecting.

The latest field to be inaugurated is Lalang, two of whose operators are the British companies BP and Lasmo, following their takeover of the Hudbay interests in Indonesia. Some 160 kilometres east of Singapore and just off the east coast of Sumatra, Lalang lies in the Malacca Straits, which are still the territory of roving pirates. The onshore oil company offices are part of the grid patterns carved out of the jungle by the development and *transmigrasi* programmes of the government.

President Suharto inaugurated the field in July 1984 from his office in the Merdeka Palace in Jakarta by means of the Palapa telecommunications satellite, another sign of the technological times. His ceremonial speech was notable for another exhortation to the state oil company Pertamina to smarten up its operations – following the traumatic replacement of its controversial president Jodo Sumbono.

Pertamina is the vehicle of the Indonesian government's oil and gas effort. Its former president Ibnu Sutowo brought the company – and the country – to the brink of extinction in 1975, when stern official efforts were made to clean up what had become the dirtiest act in town (see p. 102). But remours that all was not sanitized had been circulating in the Indonesian oil industry and in Singapore for many months before Sumbono's demise.

One of Pertamina's main tasks is to supervise and revise the production-sharing agreement with foreign oil companies, a system inaugurated by President Suharto on his accession to power. The basic terms are that Pertamina receives 85 per cent of the income from oil produced by the company, which gets the 15 per cent remainder, while the two sides agree on an annual work programme and the foreign contractor makes a commitment on minimum levels of exploration expenditures. The oil company also has to supply part of its production to Pertamina for sale on a concessionary basis and to refine part of its own crude-oil entitlement at Indonesian refineries. Pertamina has the right to sell 50 per cent of all oil produced.

The haggling and cajoling over these contracts surfaces periodically, when oil-company gripes about Pertamina, and vice versa, come to a head. In 1982–3 Pertamina was involved in tortuous negotiations with the American contractor Caltex (owned jointly by Socal and Texaco), which produced an agreement with a production-sharing ratio of 88 to 12. Caltex agreed to invest $3 billion over the eighteen years of the new contract period.

The deal was crucial since the Caltex concession in Sumatra produces over half of total Indonesian output. Its handling did nothing to allay the dismay of oil companies at the style of Sumbono. Quotes from oilmen in various companies have the same theme: 'he was not as approachable as his predecessor, not as reasonable,' says one; 'the management style was one of intimidation: his staff were running scared and it tended to inhibit action,' comments another; 'it's all bound up in bureaucracy, and he's been throwing his weight around,' says another.

Whatever the real reasons for Sumbono's dismissal, and there was talk of Sutowo-style excesses and foreign adventures, the official statement on the appointment of Abdul Rachman Ramli, the head of the state tin company, as his successor said the move was intended to promote greater efficiency at Pertamina and to enhance its role as a foreign-exchange earner.

The state oil company has never been very strong on the marketing and refining side, and Ramli will obviously have to direct his attentions to this area. But the main job will be to rebuild bridges with the foreign oilmen. Before the Caltex agreement came through, Pertamina bungled negotiations with Stanvac, the company operated by Mobil and Exxon, and had to take over its oil exploration concessions in southern Sumatra. The feeling in the Indonesian oil industry is that the state company may not be able to operate its new holdings.

In the face of complaints of 'anti-foreigner' feeling, one of the outstanding features of Pertamina's strategy for the oil industry over the next decade will be an 'Indonesianization' programme which is already under way. This will attempt to increase the number of trained indigenous workers at all levels of the oil industry. 'Trained labour is difficult to get hold of,' says one foreign oil-company executive; 'you need to pinch from someone.'

Under this government policy foreign contractors are obliged to replace their expatriates by Indonesians as trained local staff become available. Pertamina's foreign contractors are paying $100 a month for each expatriate employed in their Indonesian operations to a special fund which finances overseas courses for Indonesian students.

Oil companies wishing to stay in Indonesia are seeing the light. Hudbay recruited 45 Indonesian high-school graduates for the Lalang operation who spoke no English but were given language and technical training, in Indonesia, before joining the field staff. Some 120 students are meanwhile on training courses at American universities.

The Indonesianization scheme has several other prongs. One is that increasing pressure is being exerted on the oil companies for fabrication and other sub-contracting work to be done in Indonesia, rather than, say, Singapore. Hudbay set up its first project team for the Lalang operation in Singapore, but was told that the process had to be carried out in Indonesia. Jackets for the platforms and other necessary items are now being made on Batam Island, on which there is a fully fledged construction yard.

The increase in exploration activity and the finds now coming into production have allayed fears that Indonesia might lose its self-sufficiency in oil before the turn of the century (though consumption is running ahead of production: domestic consumption now accounts for about 40 per cent of total output). And the energy picture has brightened with the commissioning in 1984 of the Dumai refinery in Sumatra, which has made Indonesia self-sufficient in refining.

The revamping of the Dumai refinery was the third such exercise in a year, a $4 billion investment designed to match the capabilities of the refinery with the country's needs. The other two expansions were of the Cilacap plant in central Java and of the Balikpapan refinery in East Kalimantan. The new hydrocracker facility at Dumai will permit the processing of low-sulphur crude oils which previously had to be sent abroad for refining. With the use of such techniques, Indonesia could become a net exporter of refined petroleum products in the near future.

However, the coming of self-sufficiency will have serious implications for Singapore, Indonesia's sixth largest customer for oil. Indonesia's reliance on Singapore for refining will cease – and processing contracts started to be phased out in 1982.

The horse-trading in the energy sector between the countries of the region should allow this hiccough to pass. Japan, which takes half of Indonesia's oil exports, Singapore and Korea are all involved in energy deals with Indonesia whose importance could grow over the next decade, especially those involving gas.

Indonesia has been the world's largest exporter of LNG since 1980, and the oil companies are continuing to make new gas finds. But their development depends on Pertamina reaping additional sales from the aforementioned countries and from Taiwan. There has already been one spectacular success, with the signing of a new contract under which Korea will take 1.2 million tons of LNG per annum for 20 years from 1986, challenging Japan's position as the dominant customer.

But much depends on plans to invoke regional co-operation in developing new gas fields. The most grandiose scheme envisaged so far is the construction of a $7.5 billion pipeline which would link the gas reserves of northern and southern Sumatra with Batam Island and thence Singapore in the first stage; the second would be the building of a pipeline connecting the Sumatran fields with Java; and the third would be the construction of a pipeline between the huge Natuna gas basin in the South China Sea and Batam.

A study by two Dutch companies concluded that the scheme could be self-financing by fulfilling half of Singapore's gas needs initially and using the export revenues to finance other stages of the project. The pipeline network could be operational by 1987, according to this initial study.

The Dutch report was just one of several undertaken to see what could be done with the gas in Esso's East Natuna field. Esso, Pertamina and a Japanese company have all looked at the possibilities for exploiting what could be the world's largest gas field. Lee Kuan Yew has had talks with Suharto on the subject, and the Malaysians have also been discussing pipelines which might take the Indonesian gas on into the Malaysian peninsula. But much depends on Esso, which has already spent $26 million on planning and technical studies: the multinational oil companies are currently hard-headed about leaving oil or gas in the ground if markets cannot be tied up in advance for their produce.

The Indonesians are attempting to make more internal use of gas by means of a joint programme to be run by the Departments of Energy and of Industry. A methanol plant on Bunyu Island will use natural gas as its basic raw material, as will new cement and fertilizer plants. The direct-reduction units of the Krakatau Steel factory will also consume gas.

Japanese involvement in the energy sector is growing. A consortium of Japanese firms signed a $1.4 billion, 12-year contract with Pertamina for the purchase of gas, while Japan's latest, $231 million, loan to Indonesia will fund a number of projects, including an electricity distribution and transmission system in east Java. A consortium of South Korean companies has meanwhile found coal in East Kalimantan, which will soon contribute to Indonesia's expanding coal production.

The self-sufficiency *leitmotif* which appears in the energy sector will be used in other industrial areas. 'One can well put the argument that it is not an economic proposition to construct steel plants or petrochemical complexes when the world is awash with these products, but Indonesia is being nurtured as an economic giant of the future which wants its own sources of supply,' says one Western diplomat in Jakarta.

The promotion of self-sufficiency is combined with import

substitution and encouragement of NOE. The new five-year plan has an eight-point agenda for broadening and deepening the industrial base, which includes these tenets and emphasizes the development of the engineering industries, especially machinery and electronics, and of small-scale, labour-intensive industries.

While the country's manufacturing industry relies heavily at the moment on processing agricultural products, production of textiles, cement, fertilizers, metals and glass products has grown in leaps and bounds over the past few years. Now, the president is talking of self-sufficiency in a number of novel areas for Indonesia.

President Suharto has called on the cement and paper industries to reduce dependency on imports, and Indonesia will become self-sufficient in newsprint when the Leces paper mill starts production early in 1985. The state-owned cement plant in west Sumatra has recently commissioned a third unit, and the president has urged it to improve distribution so that prices may be stabilized in the face of growing industrial demand for cement.

Some of the industrial projects already under way will enable the development of industries such as machine tools to take off. The most spectacular project in the heavy-industry sphere is the Krakatau Steel project in Cilegon, west of Jakarta, which will be the first integrated steel plant in south-east Asia. Work has started on the construction of an $825 million cold-rolling steel mill, and the plant is planned to have an annual capacity of 2.2 million tonnes, with an industrial estate being built around it.

Krakatau Steel has had a chequered history, since the economics of the plant were dubious from the outset and the costs of developing the infrastructure soared during Pertamina's involvement under Ibnu Sutowo in the 1970s. An earlier Soviet-built plant has been gathering rust on the same site since the mid-1960s. However, the scheme now seems set to provide the south-east Asian and Pacific region with its own local source of steel. Similar thinking lies behind the

$2 billion Asaha aluminium project in north Sumatra – a project 75 per cent owned by Nippon Asaha Aluminium of Japan, to which aluminium will be exported.

State-owned industrial corporations like Krakatau Steel have predominated in the early efforts to build the industrial base, but this emphasis will change during the new Repelita. The role of state-owned enterprises as the motor for development diminished during the economic crisis since these corporations were heavily involved in the forty-seven projects which were rescheduled. Under the new development plan the state sector will receive only 21 per cent of government industrial investment, and the private sector will be urged to take up the remainder. There are also schemes like the campaign launched by BKPM (the Investment Co-ordinating Board) to woo private investment into the metal and engineering industries.

Foreign companies, especially those from the region, need little bidding to take up the offers which will benefit them. Suzuki is already in a joint venture to build motorbikes and cars in Jakarta, and the Japanese are also the partners in the joint-venture textile mills in west Java from which over 70 per cent of production is now being exported. The South Koreans and the Taiwanese have transferred the base of their plywood industries to Indonesia and, at the other end of industrial evolution, Fairchilds are making computer chips in the islands. The first ever joint industrial project sponsored by ASEAN was inaugurated earlier this year when the $400 million fertilizer plant at Aceh in north-west Sumatra kicked off.

Foreign industrialists working in Indonesia are enthusiastic about the schemes up to a certain point. Much of the recent development has been conducted behind high tariff barriers and other protective measures, with the result that inefficiencies have become rife in Indonesia's nascent industries, and quality control is sadly lacking in many.

Industries like textiles are thus faced with the dilemma of whether they should gear up for foreign production after saturating the local market or whether the effort would be better directed by retrenching and looking to invest elsewhere. Indonesia's textile exports, such as they are, have to compete with those from other producers in the area like India and China – whose imported products still sell well in Indonesia despite the protectionist measures. Even at this early stage of development, some of the small textile firms clustered around Bandung have begun to go under.

As the new industrial expansion gathers pace, problems like the chronic lack of local middle-level management will begin to be worrying for both the Indonesians and the foreign firms setting up there. 'All of the foreign companies here act as training schools, but the problem persists,' says one expatriate businessman in the manufacturing sector. On the other hand, says the same man, 'higher education could lead to social difficulties if graduates are deposited onto a job market where developments have not taken place'.

The other great drawback for the foreign companies looking for joint-venture opportunities under the new plan is that the BKPM has progressively reduced investment openings and may have to revise its policy in certain sectors as it is now doing in the engineering and metal industries. The laws on foreign companies not owning estates may be discussed further under the new Repelita – foreign businessmen say firms would queue up to bid for such estates – despite President Suharto's understanding of the rural Indonesian ethos and his unwillingness to offend the villagers.

For whatever the industrialization fanfares emanating from Jakarta the agricultural sector remains vital to Indonesia – and is the most successful example of efficient self-sufficiency. Indonesia has not fallen into the trap of other oil-rich developing countries like Nigeria and Mexico of neglecting its rural sector in the rush for urban, Westernized prosperity.

The Javanese are still very attached to the soil, and while

the beautifully sculpted rice terraces are owned and tilled by many more smallholders these days (to the extent where family holdings not large in themselves are now further sub-divided), there has not been the drift away from the land seen elsewhere. About two-thirds of Indonesians still live in rural areas, which employ over half the workforce. The fourth Repelita states that 'the agricultural sector will grow substantially and remain the vehicle for employment creation for years to come'; it is targeted to create 2.7 million new jobs over the next five years, and to maintain its share of over one-quarter of total GDP.

Nigeria has developed the true oil-producer's Midas touch and has had to become a major food importer since the black gold took a hold on the economy. Indonesia, in contrast, has recorded a major success story in rice production, keeping abreast of the needs of its young population by building new dams and irrigation canals in the lush terrain between the volcanoes of Java and Bali.

International agencies like the World Bank and the FAO have poured in money and assistance, and seen their assiduousness pay off. Indonesia became self-sufficient in rice production in 1982, having been the world's largest importer at one stage. By one of those vicious ironies with which the Third World is afflicted, the 1982 and 1983 crops were hit by drought, to the extent that in 1983 Indonesia had to import 1 million tonnes of rice from Thailand and Burma to cover a shortfall.

Rice production has risen to some 23 million tonnes from less than 20 million at the end of the 1960s, but there is concern now that investment in this crop is showing diminishing returns and that the agricultural sector is beginning to shed labour again. The government has been particularly alarmed at the recent trend in non-rice food crops like cassava, corn and sweet potatoes, which have seen output drop.

The new development plan will try both to increase the production of foodstuffs further – it has doubled in the last eight years – and to prevent people leaving the land. International aid officials generally feel that the farmers could produce more if they were provided with more incentives, but the crux of the problem is that Java and Bali are over-farmed: the sculpted terraces are part of an ingenious agricultural system whose main aim is to allow more and more people to get the most out of the same area of land.

Part of the official solution is highly controversial. This is the *transmigrasi* programme, which intends to disperse the teeming millions from Java and Bali to the outer islands, with priority given to farmers. Under the last five-year plan, about 2 million people were moved, and this should go up to 3–4 million over the next five years, during which time the Indonesian government intends to build 300,000 new homes throughout the archipelago to cope with the continuing population explosion.

The programme has been beset with difficulties from all sides in the past, despite government incentives such as the clearing of part of a 12.5 acre plot allocated to each settler family, the provision of household and farming equipment from official funds and the payment of a one-year subsistence allowance. On the settlers' side, moving may mean a break with animist beliefs and traditions in the family's niche in Java between the volcanoes. Once they get to Sumatra, East Kalimantan or Irian Jaya, the promises they heard from officialdom back home may translate in reality into an environment of hostile wilderness and the occasional hostile native – who may well have been shoved off his patch to make way for a Javanese.

The *transmigrasi* programme has also had ecological fall-out in the frontier areas, so much so that President Suharto was moved to warn of the dangers to rain forests of reckless forestry (and Indonesia is now one of the world's leading plywood exporters). Though President Sukarno once described these resettlement efforts as a matter of life and death for Indonesia, there has been much erosion, flooding and soil damage from the land-clearance programmes involved. Farmers used to the congested familiarity of Java are also faced with land that is less fertile – and sometimes prowled by tigers and other wild animals.

However, most of the resettled are landless peasants from the overcrowded islands, and some are homeless big-city dwellers long unaccustomed to farming. Consequently, some of the transplants from Jakarta are rejected, and many of the families fail to make a success of the move. Those who drift back to the main islands with horror stories help dissuade other potential candidates – though the government is stepping up the propaganda campaign.

This problem points up two of the prevalent social weaknesses in the islands. One is that, in common with most developing countries, Indonesia's land ownership shows a remarkable concentration in remarkably few hands, a characteristic of what is still a feudal system. The second is that the resettlement programme is seen by many non-Javanese as little short of a Javanization scheme through which the Jakarta rulers will colonize and pacify the outlying natives. The Javanese smile is said by members of other ethnic groups to be considerably more dangerous than the real jungle tiger, whose smile is a forewarning of aggression.

The Javanese way of life, its mysticism, mystery and resilience in the face of foreign influences, are now firmly entrenched as the system of Indonesian government and officialdom. Western businessmen become inured to sitting in ministerial anterooms in the usually vain hope that contracts which have been under discussion for months or even years will materialize, in waits which are punctuated by the news that this or that official has gone to the mosque.

But the tiger has been almost breaking into a smile recently as the country's development plans have been forced to tread water. The military and Golkar have worked themselves up into a sloganizing lather over the various reform programmes stemming from the economic crisis. Vigilance is again the watchword at what could be the second crucial juncture in a young nation's life.

The austerity measures pushed through in the wake of the

economic crisis may have received the approbation of Western financiers and politicians. But the 1982 election campaign (even though Suharto's re-election appeared to be no more than a formality) was marred by claims of electoral fraud and outbreaks of violence. The claims came as an élite group, the Group of 50, headed by the former minister of mines, Slanet Bratanata, called for an end to the abuses of power they claim are the staple feature of the Suharto government.

Despite the censorship of the press, periodic closures of political magazines like *Tempo* and the prevalence of informers, criticism has been mounting. Unfortunately for the dissidents, they lost one of their most powerful and internationally respected spokesmen when the former foreign minister, Adam Malik, died in September 1984. Malik had become increasingly incensed at the mysterious killings, and wrote to the president earlier in the year calling on him to put an end to the summary executions by death-squads. Just before his death, the Group of 50 published a book called *Save Democracy*.

The passage of time is even blurring the distinction between Suharto and Sukarno. But new T-shirts and stickers of the Bung (as Sukarno is affectionately called) are appearing; students who are too young to have lived through his excesses talk of the exciting persona of the former leader while dismissing the relatively colourless stage presence of Suharto.

The fight on the home front could be matched by some subtler sparring on the overseas front. The Suharto administration has always been virulently anti-Communist, and anti-Chinese feeling is still common in Java. But business links are being cultivated with the Soviets, the East Germans, and even the homeland Chinese, despite the fact that Indonesia has no official relations with China. The T-shirts sold to international beach bums in Bali may be embellished with Indonesian designs and slogans; they are manufactured in China. Thus far, America has not murmured too loudly.

The Javanese attachment to mysticism is one of the

well-springs of Suharto's presidential style, and the new industrialization may be said to be evolving from his communion with the spirits in Javanese holy places. To return to my opening analogy, a Javanese audience appreciates the legend and mysticism portrayed through the *wayang* and sits through a performance for hours in apparent contentment.

Violence between the peoples of Indonesia still simmers. General Murdhani committed troops to fresh offensives in 1984 against the guerrillas of East Timor, and there were international claims of mass civilian killings. In Jakarta in the autumn of 1984 there was also a fresh outbreak of clashes apparently between Javanese and Chinese, suggesting that the lingering resentment against the Chinese is not far beneath the surface, and that memories remain of Chinese involvement with the 'year of living dangerously'.

The recent signs of restiveness among President Suharto's captive audience could be ominous. Yet ironically the way to development may depend on the great puppeteer staying in charge for the next decade, as he plans. If he succeeds, the giant of the Pacific basin may be able to move across the stage of its own volition to assume its place in the mythology of the new industrialized world; if he fails, the *wayang* heroes and villains could be in for another violent setpiece.

Note on sources

The bulk of the information in this chapter derives from interviews with Indonesian government officials and civil servants, with foreign diplomats, businessmen and aid officials based in Jakarta, with bankers who provided invaluable insights into Indonesia's adjustment measures. Many of the economic statistics are taken from the 'Economic Update 1984' document published by the National Development Information Office in January 1984, which provides the framework for the fourth Five-Year Development Plan. General and historical background was enhanced by reading Bill Dalton's *Indonesia Handbook* (Moon Publications, P.O. Box 1696, Chico, CA, 95927, USA) and Hamish McDonald's *Suharto's Indonesia* (Fontana, London).

CONCLUSION

'The answer is yes, but remind me what the question was.'

That quote from Woody Allen popped up surprisingly in a report on 'the computerization of society' from the stuffy French bureaucracy. It was used to illustrate the point that all one can do about the more distant future is to pose a series of questions. And nowadays even 1994 becomes the distant future. A week was a long time in the politics of Harold Wilson in the 1960s; it is an age in today's acceleration of industrial change.

That, at any rate, is our joint excuse for not daring to prophesy whether south-east Asia will be the world's economic power centre of 2001 – or whether, indeed, events will move so fast that the region will have achieved and passed its peak by then and somewhere else (South America?) will be setting the pace, as some of the thinkers of Singapore suggest.

One great imponderable is China – earth's most populous land and the original home of numerate man, where the abacus was invented twenty-six centuries ago. The speed – and methods – of China's modernization will, of course, affect the world balance of power as well as the economies of her Asian neighbours. So far, trade with China has not reached major levels for any of our four sample nations, but it is quietly – sometimes almost surreptitiously – increasing.

There is a clue to both pace and method in the way in which the Chinese government is developing Guangdong province, next door to Hong Kong, as almost the reverse of the Communist coin: competitive pay rates and a trickle of Western consumer trivia are arriving with the introduction of Western technology in industry and telecommunications. The agreement on the return of Hong Kong to China in 1997 also contains elements which should allow that gateway to retain at least some of its entrepreneurial friskiness.

But, whatever way things may go, there are joint lessons to be drawn from the recent histories of Korea, Singapore, Japan and Indonesia. Before we go into those, let's remind ourselves of the disparate backgrounds that have produced such common themes:

Japan: The course-setter, not only for south-east Asia but, in some respects, for the world; a fiercely competitive nation, now striving to prove that it has the strength of inventiveness as well as the industriousness to adopt and improve upon Western technology.

South Korea: A land of mountains and real winters, the home of a hardy people who are trying to manage two industrial revolutions at the same time, building into microelectronics from a basis of traditional smoke-stack industries – ship-building, steel, cars, petro-chemicals.

Singapore: A small tropical island, with no natural resources, little heavy industry, and only 2.5 million people, predominantly Chinese, who are leap-frogging over their immediate neighbours into the post-industrial 'brain' businesses.

And Indonesia: The one exception, a troubled, divided laggard, stuffed with natural riches, yet having to struggle for unity of purpose among 160 million people spread across an archipelago of nearly 13,700 islands.

The first common theme – and a theme that compares alarmingly with the current British experience – is the emphasis on higher education. South Korea and Singapore, as much as Japan, see the need to produce graduate-crammed populations to create the wealth of the future. Those investments in the universities are aimed not merely at meeting the narrow, cannon-fodder demands for specific (and perhaps short-lived) technical skills; they seek to produce multi-disciplinary graduates, capable of handling the kaleidoscopic shifts of information-based economies and avoiding the pit of the 'two cultures' into which Britain has fallen.

The second theme is consensus, sometimes more apparent than real, but none the less providing the basis for confident national planning. The first three countries fit that pattern but, currently, Singapore supplies the sharpest example. There you see a heady hybrid of vigorously competitive capitalism and one-party state socialism (neither of those labels are really accurate, but they are the nearest fit one can find in the old-world political vocabulary of the 1980s). The government sets the strategy and invests huge sums of public money in building the infrastructure: housing, education, transport, telecommunications. The business world is then left fairly free to build the nation's wealth on that foundation. This brings us back to the quotation at the head of this chapter.

The French government's Nora Report, published in 1978 after a 12-month study ordered by President Giscard d'Estaing, became a best-seller in France and the world's most quoted official verdict on the political implications of the computer. Its recipe for ameliorating the chaos of change – and, at least, removing from the new industrial revolution the physical horrors of the first – was inevitably a broad, long-term national strategy, rooted in consensus. That is, of course, a common argument: only those nations which have middle-road agreement, whose versions of 'yo-yo' politics impinge only on the details of cutting the cake, not on how the cake is made, will be able to manage the next two decades of flux.

But the Nora Report went further. It accepted an argument of the futurologists that is still anathema to political establishments: that in a post-industrial economy both capitalism and socialism lose their meaning, because wealth is created with the minimum of capital and the minimum of labour and because all citizens can receive immediate and wide information from multiple sources. The Nora Report said that both the liberal and Marxist approaches will be 'rendered questionable' by the death of the production-based society with which they were contemporary; that the social effects of the computer are more important than its economic effects 'because they throw the traditional games of power into disorder'.

There are signs of new forms of politics emerging among our sample nations – albeit from an authoritarian start. Certainly, there is evidence (Indonesia apart, again) that their political decision-making is more effective than that of the old industrialized nations. The American pop futurologist Alvin Toffler has argued that Western governments have reached a state of 'almost total paralysis' because of political systems that were fashioned before the telephone, let alone the computer network.

When Lee Kuan Yew, in Singapore, derides the inefficiencies of one-person, one-vote democracy, he is hardly likely to be contemplating Toffler-style reforms: cumulative voting on specific issues to allow degrees of preference; or, plug-in, plug-out political parties that service the changing concerns of minorities; or legislatures chosen randomly like a jury. Yet, as the tide of the highly educated advances in countries like Korea and Singapore, their industrial discipline might evolve into new political disciplines, which avoid damaging conflicts while allowing wider individual choice.

The theme of consensus is tightly tied to common theme No. 3: the ability to manage constant change. In the purely economic battle, the new powers of south-east Asia clearly have both government mechanisms and social attitudes that enable them to cope with accelerating technological change better than the rusty structures of Western democracies and the rigid structures of Communism. And the economic impact of this adaptability is growing with the growth of international communications.

Here is one example of that global village effect: the 1983 annual survey of the Singapore Ministry of Trade and Industry noted that after substantial investment in modernization, the output of the island's printing industry had grown by 7 per cent in the year, and the survey added: 'With the help of modern satellite telecommunications facilities in Singapore, the industry was able to secure additional orders for the printing of international publications.' Some of those orders were won from Britain.

But technological change is also breeding social change, and there things do not look so certain. Even Japan is now getting itchy on several levels, though not to the extent of the Singapore Establishment's fear of 'Western values' damaging national unity. Union concern is growing in Japan that both the job-for-life guarantees for about a quarter of the work-force in the multinational corporations and the philosophy of deliberate over-manning in internal service industries may not survive the emergence of the peopleless factories and the automated offices.

There is some evidence, too – though admittedly sporadic and anecdotal – that the work ethic is becoming diluted among Japan's high-fliers. Younger executives in the multinationals, nearing the end of tours of duty in the United States or Europe, will sometimes say regretfully that they will no longer have the time when they return to Tokyo to improve their tennis or their golf, and that their children will have to become re-immersed in a pressurized education system. Such talk clearly goes deeper than the dangerous Japanese habit of saying what they think the listener wants to hear.

As long ago as October 1981 – an age in computer count – Sozaburo Okamutsa, electronics director of the Ministry of

International Trade and Industry, made some notable admissions. He was speaking at the Tokyo conference called in an attempt to get Western collaboration in creating the 'fifth generation' of computers for the 1990s; and he saw those radically more powerful computers helping to provide 'a vigorous and comfortable society', offering solutions to the 'computer allergy' emerging in Japan, to the arrival of technology-driven unemployment, and to the fears of an ageing society.

On that last count Japan has more immediate need to worry than her Asian rivals, which mostly have a younger age profile. But concern about the diminution of family responsibility and of traditional respect for the old is common to all.

It needs to be remembered also that – Japan apart – the prosperity of the new Asian powers is, in individual terms, only a richness relative to their immediate pasts. The gap between rich and poor in our sample countries is greater than it is in most West European nations. And the poor are poorer.

However, the final common theme is the most powerful of all. It is a fierce pride in national resurgence, which sometimes has its roots in history but which takes its current driving force from each nation's transformation within less than three decades. That pride could well be enough to retain national unity amid the social changes now beginning. It might even teach the rest of the world how to achieve personal liberty without divisiveness. We shall see.

It is certain, though, that the ancient Chinese benediction, which roughly translates, 'May you not have to live in interesting times', is nowadays appreciated in the West, not the East.